SAT Grammar—Prioritized

A workbook for SAT Writing

Book 2 in the

Wise Owl Tutoring

Test Prep Series

Bettie Wailes

Wise Owl Publishing, LLC

SAT Grammar—Prioritized

Wise Owl Tutoring Test Prep Series

Copyright © 2014 Bettie Wailes

Wise Owl Publishing, LLC

Winter Park, FL 32792

All rights reserved. No part of this work may be reproduced or transmitted in any form, or by any means, electronic or mechanical, without written permission form the publisher. Exceptions are made for brief excerpts to be used in published reviews.

Manufactured in the United States of America

ISNB: 978-1-938464-01-0

SAT Grammar— Prioritized

A workbook for SAT Writing

Book 2 in the

Wise Owl Tutoring

Test Prep Series

Bettie Wailes

Wise Owl Publishing, LLC

TABLE OF CONTENTS

INTRODUCTION		*iii*
1.	**Verbs**	1
1-A.	Identifying subjects and verbs	1
1-B.	Subject-verb agreement	4
1-C.	Incorrect use of "ing" verbs	9
1-D.	Verb tense: wrong tense, shift in tense, and past/past perfect tense	14
1-E.	Missing verb, incomplete sentence	20
1-F.	Active/passive verbs	25
2.	**Pronouns**	31
2-A.	Pronoun/antecedent agreement	31
2-B.	Unclear pronoun reference	35
2-C.	Shift in Point of View	40
2-D.	Nominative vs. objective case	44
2-E.	Unnecessary pronoun or no antecedent	49
2-F.	Relative pronouns: whom, which, that, when, etc.	55
3.	Dangling or Misplaced Modifiers	61
4.	Parallelism	69
5.	Wordy, Awkward, or Illogical Construction	75
6.	Wrong Word Usage	81
7.	Comma Splices/Run-on Sentences	87
8.	Wrong Comparisons	93

9.	Disagreement in Number	97
10.	Adverbs (Usually missing "ly")	99
11.	Correlative Conjunctions	101
12.	Comparative vs. Superlative	105
13.	Notes on Essay Writing	109
Appendix A: Basic Grammar Definitions		111
Appendix B: Answers to Exercises		113

INTRODUCTION

Since the introduction of the Writing section to the SAT in 2005, I realized that the essay contributes only about one-third of the total Writing score, which the Writing Multiple Choice questions contribute two-thirds. Therefore, I believe it is more important to improve grammar skills than to improve essay writing. There are, however, notes on essay writing at the end of this book.

I've analyzed the grammar sections of forty-eight SAT and PSAT test forms, tracking the frequency with which each concept appears. As I did in my first book, *SAT Words—Prioritized*, I've addressed these concepts in order of importance. The results are shown in the table below.

These practice sentences are grouped according to the type of error and order of frequency on the SAT and PSAT forms. I have created sentences with errors similar to those on actual tests. It is my belief that focused practice with each type of error will lead to higher scores on the Writing section of the PSAT and SAT. Because the concepts included here are based on standard written English, they will also benefit students in their course work in high school and college.

Verb issues account for more than one third of the questions, so this workbook begins with general verb practice. I believe if you find each verb, and then find the subject of each verb, you will have identified the heart of the sentence, and thus will better comprehend the construction of the sentence. Any other error will be easier to see.

The next most frequent category has to do with pronouns. Because verb and pronoun issues are so frequent, a large number of questions are presented here for these two categories. For some of the less frequent issues, fewer questions are presented.

There are no rhetorical skills questions included in this workbook. These are the kind of questions that accompany two to three paragraph essays. For most students, these are the easiest questions in the Writing Multiple Choice section and there are only six questions per test. Because it would have been extremely time-consuming to select essays and construct typical questions, I decided to omit these kinds of questions in this workbook.

Following are explanations and practice sentences for each of the categories listed above. The explanations are brief. If you don't understand the concept after reading the explanation, consult a grammar handbook.

Appendix A contains definitions of parts of speech.

Appendix B contains answers to all exercises.

Results of Analysis of SAT Grammar Errors

		Description of Error	Percentage of Occurrence
1.	**VERBS**		34.0%
	1-A	Identifying subjects and verbs	
	1-B	Subject-verb agreement	
	1-C	Incorrect use of "ing" verbs	
	1-D	Tense: wrong tense, shift in tense, and past/past perfect tense	
	1-E	Missing verb, incomplete sentence	
	1-F	Active/passive verbs	
2.	**PRONOUNS**		13.6%
	2-A	Pronoun/antecedent agreement	
	2-B	Unclear pronoun reference	
	2-C	Shift in Point of View	
	2-D	Nominative vs. objective case	
	2-E	Unnecessary pronoun or no antecedent	
	2-F	Relative pronouns: who, which, that, when, etc.	
3.	Dangling or misplaced modifiers		9.6%
4.	Parallelism		9.4%
5.	Wordy, awkward, or illogical construction		8.8%
6.	Wrong word usage		7.2%
7.	Comma splices/run-on sentences		7.0%
8.	Wrong Comparisons		3.2%
9.	Disagreement in number		2.4%
10.	Adverbs/adjectives (usually missing "ly")		2.2%
11.	Correlative conjunctions		2.1%
12.	Comparative vs. superlative		1.2%

1. VERBS

1-A. Identifying subject and verbs

Grammar is largely about the verbs! As you can see from the percentages shown in the table in the introduction, verb issues appear far more often than any other problem. If you identify each verb, then find the subject of that verb, you're well on your way to analyzing the sentence for most other errors.

Here are a few things to keep in mind when looking for subject-verb pairs. Verbs are usually easy to identify—they show action or a state of being. Some verbs cannot be any other part of speech other than a verb, such as the "being" verbs: *be, is, am, are, was, were, been,* and *being.* Other easy-to-recognize verbs are the helpers: *has, had, have, shall, will, may, might, should, would, could,* etc. Common action verbs are: *eat, sleep, drive, talk, play, run, study, listen, write, watch, see, throw, catch, open, close, sit, stand, start, stop,* etc.

Once you locate the verb, you then need to find the subject of that verb. To find the subject of a verb, ask who or what did the action. One hint for locating the subject of each verb is to ignore all "supporting" parts of the sentence, such as non-essential phrases set off between commas, prepositional phrases, and adjectives. In other words, find the "skeleton" or "heart" of the sentence, which is the subject and verb, and perhaps a few other words.

Example: The fish in the pond that had stripes jumped much higher than the frogs.

What is the action? *jumped* That's the word in the sentence that showed action. (A second verb is "had," but that isn't the main action in the sentence.)

Who or what jumped? fish

Then, the heart of the sentence is: fish…jumped...

"in the pond" is a prepositional phrase telling us where the fish were.

"that had stripes" is a clause that acts as an adjective to tell us which fish.

Most sentences on the SAT are complex sentences with more than one clause. In these cases, there will be several subject-verb pairs.

Example: Although she never learned to read and write, Sojourner Truth was a charismatic speaker who advocated both the abolition of slavery and the advancement of women's rights.

First verb:	learned	Who learned?	she
Second verb:	was	Who was?	Sojourner Truth

| Third verb: | advocated | Who advocated? | who, a relative pronoun referring to Sojourner Truth |

This first set of exercises involves identifying each subject and verb in these sentences.

Exercise set 1-A: Identifying subjects and verbs

Underline each verb twice, and then underline each subject once. Draw a line from each subject to its verb.

Example: I was happy that Sarah asked me to go canoeing with her, but I declined because I had another commitment.

1. Although the exact cause of the fever was never determined, modern doctors now believe that Helen suffered from meningitis.

2. Conflicts between mining operations and environmentalists have repeatedly arisen, causing Congress to reconsider legislation that prohibits mining within habitats of endangered species.

3. The senator's staff is persuaded that the announcement of the investigation, coming just days before the filing deadline, was calculated to discourage the senator from running for reelection.

4. For the remainder of her life, Annie Sullivan continued to encourage Helen's appetite for learning, providing a constant light in Helen's otherwise impenetrable darkness.

5. By today's standards, Kennedy's medical problems were severe enough to qualify him for federal disability or retirement.

6. Although I did not get my usual summer tan in Toronto, the warmth of the people there more than made up for what the climate lacked.

7. Her father found odd jobs that provided food and shelter for the family, but she never felt at home—and she never felt truly safe.

8. Despite the fact that they had traveled with hundreds of other refugees, her family was suddenly alone with strangers who spoke an unintelligible language.

9. On her first day of school, many children pointed, waved, and smiled at her, but she did not understand what they said.

10. People who dislike cats sometimes criticize them for being aloof and independent; people who are fond of cats often admire them for the same qualities.

11. The starling is such a pest in rural areas that it has become necessary to find ways of controlling the growth of its population.

12. No matter how cautiously snowmobiles are driven, they are capable of damaging the land over which they travel.

13. Since there are two pencils, a pad of paper, and a ruler on each desk, students do not have to bring their own supplies.

14. By virtue of their size and supersensitive electronics, modern radio telescopes are able to gather more waves and discriminate among them with greater precision than earlier versions could.

15. Soon after the arrival of the first visitors, many residents of the remote island thought it possible that the outside world, instead of being frightening, could be fascinating and worth exploring.

16. It was a large painting and I realized as soon as it arrived at my home that no matter how much I loved it I had no wall and no room in which to display it properly.

17. Aviation belonged to the new century in part because the engineering that went into flying machines was utterly different from that of the Industrial Revolution.

18. By attracting new industry when the old factory closed, the commissioners kept the economy of the town from collapsing.

19. Simi and Phillip were inspired to become professional writers after hearing a famous author speak about the challenges of historical research.

20. Air pollution caused by industrial fumes has been studied for years, but only recently have the harmful effects of noise pollution been explored.

1-B. Subject-verb agreement

If the subject and verb appear very close together, your ear will usually tell you if they agree.

Example: Runner eat**s** ... runner**s** eat

However, if several other words or a long phrase separates the subject and verb, you might not hear if the verb is correct. One thing that might help is that the "s" rule for verbs is the opposite than that for nouns. Most plural nouns end in "s," while singular verbs end in "s." Listen to these examples:

Examples: The *cat**s** stalk* the lizard. The *cat stalk**s*** the lizard.

Here is another hint. A compound subject takes a plural verb. In the case of two nouns joined by "or" or "nor," the verb should match the noun closer to the verb.

Examples: Neither Sally nor the twins like olives.
Neither the twins nor Sally likes olives.

Exercise set 1-B: Subject-verb agreement

Your selection should result in the most effective sentence—clear and precise, without awkwardness or ambiguity.

1. The novelist Walter Hamlin wrote about homes and gardens that <u>was directly influenced by</u> the aesthetic charms of many European cities.

    (A) was directly influenced by
    (B) was a direct influence of
    (C) were directly influenced by
    (D) were a direct influence by
    (E) were directly an influence of

2. Among the great twentieth-century authors to write about the conditions of modern <u>life were George Saxon, whose</u> novels and essays describe the quest for meaning in a rapidly changing society.

    (A) life were George Saxon, whose
    (B) life was George Saxon, whose
    (C) life were George Saxon, who in
    (D) life was George Saxon, who in his
    (E) life, George Saxon in his

3. Currently displayed at the <u>Sullivan Museum is several beautiful</u> prints from Central America depicting colorfully dressed farm workers.

    (A) Sullivan Museum is several beautiful
    (B) Sullivan Museum are the several beautiful
    (C) Sullivan Museum being several beautiful
    (D) Sullivan Museum are several beautiful
    (E) Sullivan Museum will be several beautiful

4. The bright glass sculptures of Martha Harrison <u>has received</u> critical acclaim not only in her home state, Minnesota, but also in New York.

    (A) has received
    (B) has been received
    (C) have been received
    (D) has to received
    (E) have received

5. The convenience and availability of watercolor paint account for its popularity with amateur artists.

   (A) account for its popularity
   (B) account for their popularity
   (C) accounts for its popularity
   (D) is why it is popular
   (E) are a reason for its popularity

6. The scientific writings of Edward Waters, Trevor Gould, and Robert Jenkins, which has continued the discussion of genetic issues raised by Cole Tyler, are required reading in many high schools and colleges.

   (A) which has continued
   (B) so has continued
   (C) which continuing
   (D) which have continued
   (E) which by continuing

7. The mayor's aides are convinced that the announcement of the investigation, coming just days before the filing deadline, were calculated to discourage the mayor from running for reelection.

   (A) were calculated to discourage the mayor
   (B) was calculated to discourage the mayor
   (C) were calculated in order to discourage the mayor
   (D) was being calculated to discourage the mayor
   (E) they were calculated to discourage the mayor

8. The crowds outside these two movie theaters grows larger every evening.

   (A) movie theaters grows larger
   (B) movie theaters growing larger
   (C) movie theaters grow larger
   (D) movie theaters grows in larger numbers
   (E) movie theaters grow largely

9. The mediator, having negotiated a final trade agreement between the two rival nations, were credited with helping to promote international peace.

   (A) were credited with helping to
   (B) were given credit with helping to
   (C) was credited to help to
   (D) were credited for helping to
   (E) was credited with helping to

10. The skills required for designing clothes are much more intricate than those required for making custom alterations.

    (A) are much more
    (B) is much more
    (C) were much more
    (D) would be much more
    (E) are being much more

11. Until the airplane landed, neither the chief steward nor the pilot were aware that one of the passengers had become ill.

    (A) nor the pilot were aware that
    (B) or the pilot were aware that
    (C) nor the pilot are aware that
    (D) nor the pilot was aware that
    (E) nor the pilot is aware that

12. The mistakes one makes during one's youth, regardless of how serious, is not necessarily made by one's children.

    (A) is not necessarily made
    (B) is not necessary to make
    (C) is not a necessity to be made
    (D) are not necessarily made
    (E) are not necessary to be made

13. Of the twenty-two roles in the play, mine are the smallest part.

    (A) mine are the smallest part
    (B) mine are the smaller part
    (C) mine are the smallest parts
    (D) my part is the smallest
    (E) mine is the smallest

14. Jean Valjean, since he is starving and is having no money, steals a loaf of bread early in Victor Hugo's novel, *Les Miserables*.

    (A) since he is starving and is having no money
    (B) since he was starving and is having money
    (C) because he is starving and has no money
    (D) because he is starving and he has no money
    (E) motivated by being starving and no money

15. During World War I, circulation grew for English newspapers, unprecedented in numbers.

    (A) circulation grew for English newspapers, unprecedented in
    (B) circulation of English newspapers grew to unprecedented
    (C) the circulating of English newspapers was unprecedented, it grew to
    (D) the circulation of English newspapers unprecedentedly have grown in
    (E) English newspapers' circulation has grown to unprecedented

16. Before he found his current job, Simon had spent several unhappy years working in a large textile factory where the expression of offensive jargon were as common as saying "good morning."

    (A) offensive jargon were as common
    (B) offensive jargon was as common
    (C) offensively jargon was as common
    (D) offensive jargon were as common
    (E) offensive jargon were being as common

17. A traffic light placed at an appropriate location in steady streams of traffic keep the movement of vehicles under control.

    (A) keep the movement of vehicles
    (B) keeping the movement of vehicles
    (C) is keeping the movement of vehicles
    (D) keeps under control all the movement of vehicles
    (E) keeps the movement of vehicles

18. During the last ten miles of the marathon, I passed nine others and were passed by only one runner.

    (A) and were passed by only one runner
    (B) and only one other runner passed me
    (C) and one runner had passed me
    (D) and was passed by only
    (E) and was also passed by only one other runner

19. Calcium, whose role in metabolism is not yet fully understood by the experts, appear to encourage the body's fat-burning furnace when consumed daily in recommended amounts.

    (A) appear to encourage
    (B) appearing to encourage
    (C) appears to encourage
    (D) appeared to encourage
    (E) appears to be encouraging

20. In the Gulf of Mexico off the panhandle of <u>Florida lies St. Vincent and St. George Islands</u>, which form Apalachicola Bay.

(A) Florida lies St. Vincent and St. George Islands
(B) Florida lay St. Vincent and St. George Islands
(C) Florida is lying St. Vincent and St. George Islands
(D) Florida lays St. Vincent and St. George Islands
(E) Florida lie St. Vincent and St. George Islands

1-C. Incorrect use of "ing" verbs

Beware the "ing" form of a verb on this test. The "ing" form of a verb has three different uses:
   a) a present continuous verb
   b) a noun
   c) a participle

To understand this issue, we consider the verb "sing." The conjugation of *sing* is *sing, sang, sung*. I.e., I *sing* today, I *sang* yesterday, I have *sung* in the shower for years.

The word "singing" can be used in any of the three ways listed below. All of these sentences are correct.

a) A *present continuous verb* describes an action that is occurring now.

Examples: Please do not disturb me when I am *singing*.
When I am *singing*, I cannot hear the phone.

b) A *noun*, or the name of an activity.

Examples: *Singing* is not one of my talents.
My sister has become known for her *singing*.

c) *Participle*, a form of a verb used as an adjective.

Examples: *Singing* in the car, I enjoyed my drive.
Singing too loudly, Tim didn't notice that he was off key.

On this test, however, the "ing" verb form is often used incorrectly. In some sentences, a simple present or past tense is required, but the present continuous is used. Be especially cautious about the word "being."

Example: In his address to the squad, the general urged the soldiers to both prepare well and *being* alert.

"Being" is the wrong word here. The present tense "be" is correct.

Exercise set 1-C: Incorrect use of "ing" verbs

Your selection should result in the most effective sentence—clear and precise, without awkwardness or ambiguity.

1. In an address in the summer of 1937, Roger Morrison urged his listeners to free themselves from the despair of the economy <u>and looking</u> instead to the future.

    (A) economy and looking
    (B) economy, that they should look
    (C) economy and to look
    (D) economy, but they must look
    (E) economy, but looking

2. <u>In a poignant film, the documentary describing</u> the grueling trek that hundreds of families made over the Rocky Mountains in the nineteenth century.

    (A) In a poignant film, the documentary describing
    (B) A poignant film, the documentary that described
    (C) The documentary, a poignant film describing
    (D) In a poignant film, the documentary describes
    (E) A poignant film, the documentary describes

3. Consisting of more than thirteen thousand islands displayed like <u>jewels on a dazzling necklace stringing between</u> Asia and Australia, the Republic of Indonesia is one of the most beautiful and diverse nations on Earth.

    (A) jewels on a dazzling necklace stringing between
    (B) jewels on a dazzling necklace strung over
    (C) jewels strung with a dazzling necklace between
    (D) jewels on a necklace dazzlingly stringing between
    (E) jewels on a dazzling necklace strung between

4. Because Terrell was working for three years as a teacher of animal husbandry, he felt qualified for a position as field representative for the State Department of Agriculture and Animal Husbandry.

   (A) Because Terrell was working
   (B) Terrell, working
   (C) Because of Terrell's working
   (D) Because Terrell had worked
   (E) As Terrell worked

5. The survey found that given the choice, just as many commuters would drive as would take the train or the bus.

   (A) commuters would drive as would take the train or the bus
   (B) commuters driving as taking the train or the bus
   (C) trains or buses taken by commuters as driving
   (D) by commuting would drive as taking the train or taking the bus
   (E) commuting driving as taking the train or the bus

6. Mercy Otis Warren, who resented having sewing taught to her while her brothers learned Latin, history, and mathematics, arguing that gender-based restrictions on education harmed both men and women.

   (A) Warren, who resented having sewing taught to her while her brothers learned Latin, history,
       and mathematics, arguing
   (B) Warren, who resented being taught sewing while her brothers learned
       Latin, history, and mathematics, argued
   (C) Warren, resenting sewing being taught to her while her brothers
       learned Latin, history, and mathematics, she argued
   (D) Warren, resenting how she was taught sewing while her brothers learn
       Latin, history, and mathematics, had argued
   (E) Warren resented to be taught sewing while her brothers learned Latin, history,
       and mathematics, arguing

7. New York's Rockefeller Center, some say resembling a theme park for the performing arts and entertainment, with its separate facilities for television, theater, dining, and other entertainment.

   (A) Center, some say resembling
   (B) Center, some say, resembles
   (C) Center, said by some to resemble
   (D) Center, which some say resembles
   (E) Center, with its resemblance, some say, to

8. Not unexpectedly, research shows that a essential difference <u>between an introvert and an extrovert being that one enjoys</u> being alone while the other enjoys being around other people.

    (A) between an introvert and an extrovert being that one enjoys
    (B) between introverts and extroverts is that one enjoys
    (C) between an introvert and an extrovert, one enjoys
    (D) between an introvert and an extrovert is whereas one enjoys
    (E) between an introvert and an extrovert is that one enjoys

9. The government, presently constructing several complex facilities to accommodate the upcoming world-wide sporting event, <u>and hoping to transform them later to be used by vacationers</u>.

    (A) and hoping to transform them later to be used by tourists
    (B) in hopes of transform them later to be used by tourists
    (C) hopes to transform them later for tourists to use
    (D) hoping they can be transformed for tourist use later
    (E) the hope is that tourists use them later as transformed

10. Quinones yearns so deeply to see improvements in the lives of the <u>workers, having dedicated himself, therefore</u> to advancing their cause.

    (A) workers, having dedicated himself, therefore
    (B) workers that he has dedicated himself
    (C) workers, thus dedicating himself
    (D) workers so as to dedicate himself
    (E) workers, because of which he has dedicated himself

11. The old cowboy actor remains the only one of all the western genre actors in that studio <u>who is still caring about</u> the preservation of the West.

    (A) who is still caring about
    (B) who still care about
    (C) who still caring about
    (D) who still cares about
    (E) who still does cares about

12. This old sailboat that Sandy and I used is the only one of these many sailboats <u>that makes me</u> nostalgic for old times.

    (A) that makes me
    (B) that making me
    (C) that is making me
    (D) that had made me
    (E) that was making me

13. Terrence Johnson, a soul jazz trumpet player of the 1950s, <u>often departed from his usual musical structures when collaborating with</u> experimental jazz musicians.

    (A) often departed from his usual musical structures when collaborating with
    (B) often departed from his usual musical structures when he collaborated with
    (C) often departed from his usual musical structures when he was collaborating with
    (D) he often departs from his usual musical structures when collaborating with
    (E) when he collaborated, often departs from his usual soul jazz structures with

14. Customer <u>surveys revealing that a prime concern</u> of airline passengers, nearly as important as arriving on time, is receiving accurate updates from the airline.

    (A) surveys revealing that a prime concern
    (B) surveys reveal that a prime concern
    (C) surveys reveals that a prime concern
    (D) surveys are revealing that a prime concern
    (E) surveys were revealing that a prime concern

15. For several administrations, polls have indicated that <u>presidents are showing to be less popular</u> with the public that their wives.

    (A) presidents are showing to be less popular
    (B) presidents are showed to be less popular
    (C) presidents are showed as less popular
    (D) presidents will be less popular
    (E) presidents are less popular

16. George Frederick Handel, the German-born English composer of the eighteenth century, <u>is best known for his oratorios</u>, such as *Messiah* and *Solomon*.

    (A) is best known for his oratorios
    (B) is best knowing for his oratorios
    (C) are best known for his oratorios
    (D) will be best known for his oratorios
    (E) is best knew for his oratorios

17. Sonya received a D on the math test because instead of studying the night <u>before she was watching</u> a video.

    (A) before she was watching
    (B) before she watches
    (C) before she had watched
    (D) before she watched
    (E) before she watching

18. We will not go along with your plan for disrupting the city council's meeting; we will oppose it with every possible means at our disposal.

    (A) your plan for disrupting the city council's meeting
    (B) your plan for the disruption of the city council's meeting
    (C) your plan for disruption the city council's meeting
    (D) your plan to disrupting the city council's meeting
    (E) your plan to disrupt the city council's meeting

19. From Maine in the North to Georgia in the South the eastern seacoast is filling with fascinating reminders of the War of Independence.

    (A) the eastern seacoast is filling with
    (B) the eastern seacoast are filled with
    (C) the eastern seacoast is filled with
    (D) the eastern seacoast is once filled with
    (E) the eastern seacoast will be filled with

20. An Amish farmer in his horse and buggy slowly travels the long road into town to sell his produce and buying supplies.

    (A) travels the long road into town to sell his produce and buying supplies
    (B) travels the long road into town to sell his produce and buy supplies
    (C) travels the long road into town for selling his produce and buying supplies
    (D) traveling the long road into town for to sell his produce and buy supplies
    (E) traveling the long road into town to sell his produce and buy supplies

1-D. Verb Tense: wrong tense, shift in tense, and past/past perfect tense

To make sure that each verb is in the correct tense, pay attention to other verbs in the sentence and to what the sentence is about. For example, if the sentence is about an event in the eighteenth century, the verb cannot be in the future tense.

Example: The watercolor painting, one of my favorites, never fails to make me smile every time I *looked* at it.

The first verb, *fails*, is present tense, so *looked* should be present tense *look*.

Occasionally, you need to know if the verb tense should be a simple past tense or the past perfect tense. Most of the time, we use a simple **past tense**.

Example: Josh *drove* to Tallahassee last Friday to visit FSU.

However, we use the **past perfect tense** for two reasons:

    a) To show that one event happened before another event in the past.

    b) To indicate that something occurred repeatedly, or over a period of time. The past perfect tense requires a helping verb, usually had, has, or have.

a) An event that occurred before another event in the past.

Example: Josh *had driven* to Gainesville before he realized he forget his phone.

It would be awkward to say, Josh *drove* Gainesville before he …

b) An event that occurred repeatedly or over a period of time.

Example: Madison *had played* on that tennis court for years before it was destroyed by the flood.

If we said, "Madison played on that tennis court for years before…" we would be saying that Madison was playing continuously for years. Didn't she get tired? Did she set a record? Wrong meaning.

If we need the past perfect tense, we need to be sure to use the correct form of the verb. You might remember lists of irregular verbs, showing the present, past, and past perfect forms.

Most verbs form the past tense and past perfect tense by adding "ed." For example, "play" is a regular verb.

Example: I *play* today.
                I *played* yesterday.
                I *had played* in the park for years.

Many common verbs do **not** form the past and past perfect tenses in this way, though. These verbs are called "irregular" because they do not conform to any particular rule.

Examples are:

Present	*Past*	*Past Participle*
run	ran	run
swim	swam	swum
drive	drove	driven
write	wrote	written
arise	arose	arisen
eat	ate	eaten
ride	rode	ridden
hit	hit	hit

sit	sat	sat
draw	drew	drawn
sleep	slept	slept
cut	cut	cut

Lie/lay. Now we must address the dreaded "lie" and "lay," among the most confusing verbs in English. "To lie" means to recline one's body, while "to lay" means to place an object. Thus, the verb "lay" requires a direct object, the object being placed. (See Direct Object in Appendix A.) Because the present continuous tense has also appeared on the SAT, it is included here.

Present	*Past*	*Past Participle*	*Present Continuous*
lie	lay	lain	lying
lay	laid	laid	laying

Example sentences for each verb form are:

lie: Present: Because I'm sleepy, I'll *lie* down.
       Past: Yesterday, when I had a headache, I *lay* down.
       Past Perfect: I had *lain* on the floor for two hours before the paramedics arrived.
       Pres. Cont.:   I am *lying* under the umbrella in order to avoid sunburn.

lay: Present: To get ready for dinner, I'll *lay* the plates on the table.
       Past: I *laid* the book on the top shelf.
       Past Perfect: I had *laid* my calculator in the same spot for more than a year.
       Pres. Cont.:   Sharon is *laying* a blanket on the grass under the tree for our picnic.

The following sentences contain either a shift in tense or the use of the past tense that should be past perfect, and vice versa. See if you can find the error in verb tense in the following sentences.

Exercise set 1-D: Verb tense: wrong tense, shift in tense and past/past perfect tense

Choose the answer that results in a clear and concise sentence, free from awkwardness or ambiguity.

1. Many people enjoy feeding birds at a backyard feeder in the winter because the sight of cardinals and chickadees <u>was a reminder that spring is</u> just around the corner.

    (A) was a reminder that spring is
    (B) was reminding that spring is
    (C) is a reminder that spring was
    (D) is a reminder that spring is
    (E) was a reminder that spring will be

2. That beautiful roan horse is <u>one of the horses stabled here that recognized me</u> when I come up to the fence.

    (A) one of the horses stabled here that recognized me
    (B) one of the horses stabled here that will recognize me
    (C) one of the horses stabled here that recognizing me
    (D) one of the horses stabled here that recognize me
    (E) one of the horses stabled here that recognizes me

3. The Human Genome Project, a thirteen-year international collaborative research <u>program, is initiated in</u> 1990.

    (A) program, is initiated in
    (B) program, was initiated in
    (C) program, had been initiated in
    (D) program, will be initiated in
    (E) program, that was being initiated in

4. After <u>they identified and eliminate potential sources</u> of toxins, the renovators plan to restore the historic home with environmentally safe materials.

    (A) they identified and eliminate potential sources
    (B) they identified and eliminated potential sources
    (C) they identify and eliminated potential sources
    (D) they identified, as well as eliminate potential sources
    (E) they identify and eliminate potential sources

5. After the League of Women Voters was organized in 1920, <u>it announces twin goals</u>: to encourage women to exercise their right to vote and to educate others about social and political issues.

    (A) it announces twin goals
    (B) it announced twin goals
    (C) it was announcing twin goals
    (D) the twin goals it announces
    (E) it is announcing twin goals

6. The League is proud to be nonpartisan, never having supported or opposed candidates or political parties at any level of government, <u>but always working on vital issues</u> of concern to member and the public.

    (A) but always working on vital issues
    (B) but always to be working on vital issues
    (C) but always worked on vital issues
    (D) but always will work on vital issues
    (E) but has always worked on vital issues

7. Dr. Seuss, whose many books have sold in the millions, have made him probably the best-selling children's author in history.

    (A) have made him
    (B) has made him
    (C) made him
    (D) thereby making him
    (E) is

8. The Food and Drug Administration has overlooked the dangers of some drugs that seemed perfectly safe until long after they are in general use.

    (A) they are in general
    (B) they were in general
    (C) they were being in general
    (D) they had been in general
    (E) they are in general

9. Plato and Aristotle taught that the supreme human being is the philosopher—the person of reason who looked upon life with dispassion.

    (A) who looked upon life
    (B) who looks upon life
    (C) who had looked upon life
    (D) who will look upon life
    (E) who has been looking upon life

10. Praised for her soulful voice, Mamie Smith had rose to fame in the 1920s as America's premier blues singer.

    (A) had rose to fame
    (B) risen to fame
    (C) rose to fame
    (D) had risen to fame
    (E) rose up to fame

11. His experience writing legal thrillers served John Grisham well when he writes the screenplays for movies such as *The Firm* and *The Pelican Brief*.

    (A) when he writes the screenplays
    (B) when he had written the screenplays
    (C) when he had wrote the screenplays
    (D) when he wrote the screenplays
    (E) when he is writing the screenplays

SAT Grammar—Prioritized   19

12. When the workers finally rebelled against practices of the management, issues that had been ignored for years <u>suddenly assume</u> new importance.

    (A) suddenly assume
    (B) suddenly assumes
    (C) suddenly had assumed
    (D) suddenly assumed
    (E) with suddenness assumed

13. Sam Cooke composed "A Change is Gonna Come," <u>thought by some to be the best</u> protest song of the 1960s.

    (A) thought by some to be the best
    (B) has thought by some to be the best
    (C) thought by some to have been the best
    (D) thought by some as the best
    (E) thought by some it is the best

14. If <u>you had kept your mistakes</u> in mind, they will often guide you to make better decisions.

    (A) you had kept your mistakes
    (B) you were keeping your mistakes
    (C) you kept your mistakes
    (D) you will keep your mistakes
    (E) you keep your mistakes

15. Although some of the victories of the women's movement of the 1970s were only token gains, many <u>others have been definite steps</u> toward workplace equality.

    (A) others have been definite steps
    (B) others are definite steps
    (C) others will be definite steps
    (D) others are considered definite steps
    (E) others were definite steps

16. Each piece of the mosaic was individually selected and positioned according to a preconceived pattern until the entire floor of the villa <u>is decorated</u>.

    (A) is decorated
    (B) has been decorated
    (C) was decorated
    (D) was with decoration
    (E) was being decorated

17. Feeling disenfranchised by a voting process that ultimately led to their votes being invalidated, these <u>citizens have shown their discontent</u> with a lawsuit.

    (A) citizens have shown their discontent
    (B) citizens showed their discontent
    (C) citizens are showing their discontent
    (D) citizens show their discontent
    (E) citizens have showed their discontent

18. Nelson expected to dislike venison, but he was pleased that the spicy <u>sauce makes it</u> quite palatable.

    (A) sauce makes it
    (B) sauce have made it
    (C) sauce were making it
    (D) sauce make it
    (E) sauce made it

19. It turns out that the task of developing test questions <u>is much more</u> demanding than that of proof-reading those questions.

    (A) is much more
    (B) had proven to be much more
    (C) are much more
    (D) was proven to be much more
    (E) will have proved to be much more

20. No matter how <u>cautiously snowmobiles have been driven,</u> they are capable of damaging the land over which they travel.

    (A) cautiously snowmobiles have been driven
    (B) cautious snowmobiles are driven
    (C) cautiously snowmobiles had been driven
    (D) cautiously snowmobiles are driven
    (E) cautiously snowmobiles have been drove

1-E: Missing verb, incomplete sentence

The verb is the only required part of speech in a sentence. Some sentences are incomplete because they do not have a proper verb and others are incomplete because there isn't a main clause.

Example: While in Greece this summer, my sister and I walking through the Coliseum.

SAT Grammar—Prioritized

Since the event has already happened, the two people aren't still walking. It should be "walked." There is no proper verb. Notice that the incorrect verb in this sentence is an "ing" verb.

Other sentences are incomplete because have one or more subordinate clauses, but no main clause. A clause that begins with a subordinating conjunction (such as *because, since, while, when, although, but, even though,* etc.) is not a main, or independent, clause.

Example: "I'll be late" is a complete sentence, but "Because I'll be late" is not.

When we begin a clause with a subordinating conjunction, it becomes a dependent clause, or a clause that must be attached to an independent clause.

Example: Although I had finished with the lawn, but I found more weeds.

Even though we see two subject-verb pairs—"I had finished" and "I found"—neither is in an independent clause. We need to drop either "although" or "but" to make one of the clauses an independent clause.

Exercise set 1-E: Missing verb, incomplete sentence

Choose the answer that results in a clear and concise sentence, free from awkwardness or ambiguity.

1. The term "doublespeak" <u>referring to the intentional use of language</u> to confuse or to mislead, as when one says "revenue enhancement' instead of "tax increase."

    (A) referring to the intentional use of language
    (B) referring to language which is intentionally used
    (C) which refers to the intentional use of language
    (D) refers to the intentional use of language
    (E) that refers to the intentional use of language

2. <u>Since some</u> people are <u>convinced that</u> warts <u>are caused by frogs</u>, but others realize that warts
       A   B   C
   <u>are the result</u> of a virus. <u>No error</u>
          D   E

3. *Things Fall Apart*, Chinua Achebe's novel about both the <u>good and the bad</u> of a village in
                                                                                              A
   nineteenth-century Nigeria, <u>which is studied</u> frequently <u>in both</u> high school and college
                                                B   C
   literature <u>courses</u>. <u>No error</u>
                     D   E

4. Even though the movie *Clueless* closely parallels Jane Austen's *Emma* and some viewers find the movie difficult to follow.

   (A) *Clueless* closely parallels Jane Austen's *Emma* and some viewers find
   (B) *Clueless* closely parallels Jane Austen's *Emma* and even though some viewers find
   (C) *Clueless* closely parallels Jane Austen's *Emma,* some viewers find
   (D) *Clueless* with its close parallel to Jane Austen's *Emma* and with some viewers finding
   (E) *Clueless,* a close parallel to Jane Austen's *Emma,* some viewers who find

5. Most recognized artists are gifted in only a single field; Gregory Walters, however, who has shown considerable talent in music, film, and photography.

   (A) single field; Gregory Walters, however, who has shown
   (B) single field; Gregory Walters, nevertheless, showing
   (C) single field; Gregory Walters, however, who has shown
   (D) single field, despite what Gregory Walters has shown
   (E) single field, but Gregory Walters has shown

6. The revered Peruvian site of Machu Picchu, abandoned by the Inca, reclaimed by the wilderness, and lost to history until it was rediscovered in 1911 and unearthed.

   (A) Picchu, abandoned by the Inca,
   (B) Picchu was abandoned by the Inca,
   (C) Picchu having been abandoned by the Inca,
   (D) Picchu, had been abandoned by the Inca, as well as
   (E) Picchu, abandoned by the Inca;

7. All the demands on soprano Kathleen Battle for operatic performances, solo concerts, and special guest appearances tempting her to sing too often and strain her voice.

   (A) tempting her to sing too often
   (B) tempted her to sing too often
   (C) were tempting her to sing too often
   (D) tempts her to sing too often
   (E) tempt her into singing too often

8. New Zealand's Kaikoura Peninsula, a ruggedly beautiful spit of land, borders an undersea canyon that is home to the sperm whale and the giant squid.

   (A) borders an undersea canyon
   (B) bordering an undersea canyon,
   (C) and it borders an undersea canyon, which is
   (D) which borders an undersea canyon,
   (E) is the border of an undersea canyon, being

SAT Grammar—Prioritized   23

9. The iris, the colored part of the eye, which contains delicate patterns that are unique to each person, offering a powerful means of identification.

    (A) which contains delicate patterns that are unique
    (B) contains delicate patterns, the ones that are unique
    (C) contain delicate patterns that are unique
    (D) contains delicate patterns that are unique
    (E) that contain delicate patterns that are unique

10. Frequently on tour, a band called the Chieftains revered internationally as spirited performers of traditional Irish music.

    (A) revered internationally as spirited performers
    (B) revered internationally and they are spirited performers
    (C) is revered internationally for its spirited performances
    (D) is revered internationally as giving spirited performances
    (E) are revered internationally as being spirited performers

11. Perhaps feeling that their votes do not matter, young people, who in increasingly smaller numbers are going to the polls.

    (A) young people, who in increasingly smaller numbers are going to the polls
    (B) young people are going to the polls in increasingly smaller numbers
    (C) the number of young people going to the polls are becoming increasingly smaller
    (D) the number of young people going to the polls is increasingly smaller
    (E) increasingly smaller numbers of young people are going to the polls

12. Josephine Baker, one of the most versatile performers of the twentieth century, and who acquired fame as a dancer, singer, Broadway actress, and move star.

    (A) and who acquired
    (B) she has acquired
    (C) and she has acquired
    (D) who acquired
    (E) acquired

13. When mammals hibernate, and their body temperatures fall to slightly above that of the
                          A   B   C   D
    surrounding air. No error
                     E

14. The editor would not print an article based on mere conjecture; because she directed the
                  A   B   C
    reporter to find convincing proof. No error
             D   E

15. So that he could end his lecture on time, <u>since Professor Percy decided to waive</u> his final point and address it instead at the next class meeting

    (A) since Professor Percy decided to waive
    (B) since he, Professor Percy decided to waive
    (C) Professor Percy decided to waive
    (D) Professor Percy has decided to waive
    (E) Professor waived

16. As the newspaper grew in circulation, salaries rose, <u>and while the older men retained</u> editorial control of the newspapers.

    (A) and while the older men retained
    (B) and while the older men had retained
    (C) and while the older men were retaining
    (D) while the older men retained
    (E) while the older men retain

17. Although other European <u>states broke apart</u> under the <u>stresses of political</u> upheaval, <u>but the</u>
                                                     A   B   C
    seventeenth-century Dutch <u>republic proved remarkably</u> resilient. <u>No error</u>
                                    D   E

18. The letter, written by a homeowner and published in the *Johnstown Chronicle*, <u>and a scathing criticism against</u> the city's handling of road repair.

    (A) and a scathing criticism against
    (B) it was a scathing criticism against
    (C) had been a scathing criticism against
    (D) were a scathing criticism against
    (E) was a scathing criticism against

19. During his Olympic career, Carl <u>Lewis, who broke several</u> world records in track.

    (A) Lewis, who had broken several
    (B) Lewis was breaking several
    (C) Lewis, who broke several
    (D) Lewis, he broke several
    (E) Lewis broke several

20. Trump Tower <u>, a New York City skyscraper in uptown Manhattan, whose importance as an architectural landmark</u> is not equal to that of the Empire State Building and The Chrysler Building.

   (A) Trump Tower, a New York City skyscraper in uptown Manhattan, whose importance as an architectural landmark
   (B) Trump Tower, a New York City skyscraper in uptown Manhattan and whose importance as an architectural landmark
   (C) Trump Tower is a New York City skyscraper in uptown Manhattan whose importance as an architectural landmark
   (D) Trump Tower, a New York City skyscraper in uptown Manhattan, important as an architectural landmark
   (E) Trump Tower, a New York City skyscraper in uptown Manhattan, being in importance as an architectural landmark

1-F. Active/passive verbs

Active verbs show an action, while passive verbs show a state of being. Active verbs are preferred. In other words, readers prefer to read "Isaac Newton developed theories" rather than "Theories were developed by Isaac Newton." In the first sentence *Newton developed*, showing us clear action. The second sentence is weaker, since *theories* is the subject, *were* is the verb (a verb of being) and we don't hear about Newton until the end.

The verbs of being (*be, is, am, are, was, were, been, being*) are passive and are considered weak verbs. Active verbs are considered strong verbs.

Example: The long-awaited completion of the transcontinental railroad in May of 1869 is why the age of tourism to the American West was ushered in.

This is poorly constructed, partly because of the weak passive verbs *is* and *was*.

Better: The long-awaited completion of the transcontinental railroad in May of 1869 ushered in the age of tourism to the American West.

Now we see action. The completion . . . ushered. . . No need for the passive *is* and *was*.

Whenever possible, use an active verb.

Exercise set 1-F: Active/Passive verbs

Choose the answer that results in a clear and concise sentence, free from awkwardness or ambiguity.

1. Cartoon detective Dick Tracy was created by Chester Gould in 1931.

    (A) Cartoon detective Dick Tracy was created by Chester Gould in 1931.
    (B) Chester Gould created cartoon detective Dick Tracy in 1931.
    (C) Cartoon detective Dick Tracy has created by Chester Gould in 1931.
    (D) Created in 1931 by Chester Gould is cartoon detective Dick Tracy.
    (E) Cartoon detective Dick Tracy, he was created by Chester Gould in 1931.

2. The potholes in the Hampton Heights neighborhood were repaired by the county.

    (A) The potholes in the Hampton Heights neighborhood were repaired by the county.
    (B) The potholes, while repaired by the county, were in the Hampton Heights neighborhood.
    (C) Because the potholes in the Hampton Heights neighborhood were repaired by the county.
    (D) The county repaired the potholes in the Hampton Heights neighborhood.
    (E) The potholes in the Hampton Heights neighborhood has been repaired by the county.

3. If you want to be the best, sacrifices must be made by you.

    (A) sacrifices must be made by you
    (B) sacrifices must be willing to be made by you
    (C) one must make sacrifices
    (D) you must make sacrifices
    (E) sacrifices are necessary to make

4. Researchers tend to praise studies that agree with their own conclusions, and it is rare for kindness to be shown to contrary theories.

    (A) conclusions, and it is rare for kindness to be shown
    (B) conclusions, and kindness being rarely shown
    (C) conclusions, and they rarely show kindness
    (D) conclusions, and they are rarely kind
    (E) conclusions, although rarely is kindness to be shown

5. Because their flight was missed, the bride's parents ran frantically to another part of the airport to catch another plane.

    (A) Because their flight was missed, the bride's parents ran
    (B) After their flight was missed, the bride's parents ran
    (C) Their flight was missed, which is why the bride's parents ran
    (D) Missing their flight, the bride's parents ran
    (E) Because they missed their flight, the bride's parents ran

SAT Grammar—Prioritized   27

6. The mountain's summit having been reached, the climbers enjoyed the view while they rested.

    (A) The mountain's summit having been reached,
    (B) The summit of the mountain having been reached,
    (C) After they reached the mountain's summit,
    (D) At the mountain's summit, when they reached it,
    (E) The mountain's summit reached,

7. When, after bleak and lonely years in an English public school, he returned to India, there was suddenly perceived by himself a strong desire to write about the people and land he loved.

    (A) there was suddenly perceived by himself
    (B) he was perceived
    (C) suddenly the feeling that came to him being
    (D) he suddenly felt
    (E) suddenly he had the feeling of

8. After author Ellie White Feather wrote down many Lakota folktales, and a novel was written by her that takes place in a nineteenth-century Lakota community.

    (A) folktales, and a novel was written by her
    (B) folktales and write a novel
    (C) folktales, and a novel was wrote by her
    (D) folktales, she also wrote a novel
    (E) folktales and had written a novel

9. After the tournament, the coach will praise the best players and a lecture will be given to the remainder of the team.

    (A) will praise the best players and a lecture will be given to
    (B) will praise the best players and then a lecture will be given to
    (C) will praise the best players and lecture
    (D) will praise the best players, along with giving a lecture to
    (E) will praise the best players, a lecture will be given to

10. The charcoal for the barbecue was supplied by the park rangers.

    (A) The charcoal for the barbecue was supplied by the park rangers.
    (B) The park rangers supplied the charcoal for the barbecue.
    (C) The charcoal was supplied by the park rangers for the barbecue.
    (D) The charcoal for the barbecue were supplied by the park rangers.
    (E) The charcoal, supplied by the park rangers, was at the barbecue.

11. The tornado tore through the outskirts of the town, toppling small buildings, uprooting trees, and power lines were snapped.

    (A) power lines were snapped
    (B) power lines was snapped
    (C) snapped power lines
    (D) power lines snapped
    (E) snapping power lines

12. When I prepare a new recipe, I first gather utensils and ingredients, and then those ingredients are mixed as I follow the instructions.

    (A) ingredients, and then those ingredients are mixed
    (B) ingredients, mixing those ingredients then
    (C) ingredients and then I mix those ingredients
    (D) ingredients, then I mix these ingredients
    (E) ingredients, I mix those ingredients then

13. Unlike many English prime ministers before him, deep insight into the workings of the human mind was had by Winston Churchill.

    (A) deep insight into the workings of the human mind was had by Winston Churchill
    (B) deep insight into the workings of the human mind was held by Winston Churchill
    (C) deep insight into the workings of the human mind were held by Winston Churchill
    (D) deep insight by Winston Churchill was held into the workings of the human mind
    (E) Winston Churchill had deep insight into the workings of the human mind

14. Underhandedness was used by Fred to achieve his professional goals.

    (A) Underhandedness was used by Fred
    (B) Fred used underhandedness
    (C) Underhandedness were to be used by Fred
    (D) Underhandedness were used by Fred
    (E) Underhandedness, used by Fred

15. The furnace exploded, blowing off the door, spraying greasy soot all over the basement floor, and the furniture and windowpanes were rattled throughout the building.

    (A) and the furniture and windowpanes were rattled throughout the building
    (B) and rattling furniture and windowpanes throughout the building
    (C) and throughout the building the furniture and windowpanes were rattled
    (D) and the furniture and windowpanes was rattled throughout the building
    (E) and rattling of the furniture and windowpanes throughout the building

16. After the game, the players on the winning team were congratulated by the coach.

    (A) the players on the winning team were congratulated by the coach
    (B) the players on the winning team was congratulated by the coach
    (C) the coach congratulated the players on the winning team
    (D) the players on the winning team were being congratulated by the coach
    (E) the players on the winning team had been congratulated by the coach

17. Because Tony Williams paved the way of jazz-fusion musicians who came later, he is considered an originator of that style.

    (A) Because Tony Williams paved the way of jazz-fusion musicians who came later,
    (B) Because of Tony Williams paving the way of jazz-fusion musicians who came later,
    (C) Because the way of jazz-fusion musicians who came later was paved by drummer Tony Williams,
    (D) Because the way of jazz-fusion musicians who had came later was paved by drummer Tony Williams,
    (E) Because the way of jazz-fusion musicians who were to come later was paved by drummer Tony Williams,

18. To complete the music program, a student must present one vocal performance, one instrumental performance, and one original work is composed.

    (A) and one original work is composed
    (B) and one original work
    (C) and composing one original
    (D) and one original work must be composed
    (E) and have composed one original

19. Because the bearded dragon lizard is a voracious eater, as many insects as possible are consumed by it.

    (A) as many insects as possible are consumed by it
    (B) as many insects as possible are to be consumed by it
    (C) as many insects as possible were consumed by it
    (D) it will consume as many insects as possible
    (E) it will have consumed as many insects as possible

20. More water is carried by the Amazon River than any other river in the world.

   (A) More water is carried by the Amazon River
   (B) More water, carried by the Amazon River
   (C) More water was carried by the Amazon River
   (D) The Amazon River has been carrying more water
   (E) The Amazon River carries more water

2. PRONOUNS

A pronoun is a word that stands for a person or a thing. The word that the pronoun stands for is called the antecedent. *Every pronoun must have an antecedent.*

2-A. Pronoun/antecedent agreement

In some sentences on the SAT, a singular pronoun is used to refer to a plural word, or vice versa. In some of the following sentences, the pronoun doesn't agree with its antecedent.

It is common to hear a person of unknown gender referred to as "they," but according to the standard rules of English, this is not correct. Included in this category are sentences that refer to a company, team, government, etc. as "they." These are considered single entities and should be referred to as "it."

Look to see what word the pronoun stands for and make sure that the pronoun matches the word, especially with respect to singular/plural.

NOTE: An entity such as a school, government, company, or team is considered singular.

Example: The *team* selected *its* colors forty years ago.

Example: The *company* takes pride in *its* recycling program; it has collected three tons of glass, aluminum, and paper in the last ten years.

Example: We are expecting the speaker for our meeting; *he* or *she* should arrive soon.

Exercise set 2-A: Pronoun/antecedent agreement

Choose the answer that results in a clear and concise sentence, free from awkwardness or ambiguity.

1. Masks <u>used by</u> a certain Indian tribe in Canada have interchangeable parts that <u>allow</u> the
           A   B
 wearers <u>to change</u> <u>its expression</u> during dramatic dance presentations. <u>No error</u>
            C   D   E

2. Nursery owners <u>who grow</u> foliage know that in <u>unseasonably</u> cold weather they must protect
                     A   B
 their plants from <u>potentially killing frost</u> <u>by providing it</u> with extra sources of heat. <u>No error</u>
                         C   D   E

3. When, in the early 1600s, early settlers discovered the cranberry, they were more durable than many other fruits and were taken on ships to prevent scurvy.

    (A) they were more durable than many other fruits and were taken on ships to prevent scurvy
    (B) they were taken on ships to prevent scurvy because they were more durable
    (C) being more durable than many other fruits, they were able to be taken on ships to prevent scurvy
    (D) they found it to be more durable than many other fruits, it could be taken on ships to prevent scurvy
    (E) they found that it was more durable than many other fruits and could be taken on ships to prevent scurvy

4. Aerobic activities such as running and swimming are undeniably beneficial to one's health;
                                                                   A   B   C
    even so, many people find it boring. No error
                          D   E

5. Although we may think of China as one huge country, they are a land of 56 distinct
                                          A   B
    nationalities, only some of which are ethnically related to cultural groups found elsewhere in
                      C   D
    Central and Southeast Asia. No error
                                E

6. Fallen leaves smother emerging grass and so should be kept off the lawn, but it provides the
                                A   B   C
    perfect insulation against cold and frost when used as mulch for flowers and shrubs. No error
                  D   E

7. The blue whale's body appears to be long and streamlined, and its head alone makes up almost one-fourth of their total body length.

    (A) head alone makes up almost one-fourth of their total body length
    (B) almost one-fourth of their total body length is made up by their heads alone
    (C) head alone makes up almost one-fourth of its total body length
    (D) head alone that makes up almost one-fourth of its total body length
    (E) head alone making up almost one-fourth of the total length of their bodies

8. Every building within a three-mile radius of the epicenter had an interruption in their electric service immediately following the most recent earthquake.

   (A) had an interruption in their electric service
   (B) had its electric service interrupted
   (C) had their electric service interrupted
   (D) that interrupted the electric service
   (E) that had its electric service interrupted

9. Because the Blue Whale restaurant draws so many diners, servers there are extremely busy and
                                            A   B
   seldom have a chance to sit and rest his or her feet. No error
                        C   D   E

10. Although a far more eloquent speaker, the incumbent made fewer specific suggestions in his
                    A   B
    campaign speech than the opponent did in hers. No error
                    C   D   E

11. Crickets produce their distinctive chirp by grating its right forewing across a series of ridges on its left forewing.

    (A) Crickets produce their distinctive chirp
    (B) A cricket produces their distinctive chirp
    (C) The distinctive chirp of crickets are produced
    (D) The cricket's distinctive chirp, produced
    (E) The cricket produces its distinctive chirp

12. When astronauts view Earth from space, he or she sees what seems to be a blue marble
                                 A   B   C
    suspended against a black nothingness. No error
    D   E

13. The western horned owl, which has yellow eyes, brown stripes, and feathered toes,
                            A
    is characterized by the ear-like tufts of feathers that project above their ears. No error
    B   C   D   E

14. The jet-black color of the crow <u>helps</u> <u>them</u> recognize other crows <u>at great distances</u> during the
                                      A   B   C
    day <u>while also</u> providing defense from enemies at night. <u>No error</u>
         D   E

15. <u>Between</u> 1990 and 2000, real estate developers <u>constructed</u> over a million dwellings <u>a year,</u>
    A   B   C
    most <u>of it</u> suburban single-family homes. <u>No error</u>
          D   E

16. While a mother bird broods her eggs, she turns <u>each egg every day, sometimes more often, to keep it</u> evenly warmed.

    (A) each egg every day, sometimes more often, to keep it
    (B) each egg every day, sometimes more often, so they are kept
    (C) each egg daily, and sometimes more, which kept them
    (D) each egg daily, sometimes more often, and this keeps it
    (E) each egg every day, sometimes more often, to keep them

17. New solar-powered robots, <u>unlike most of his predecessors,</u> can actually learn to walk by means of trial and error.

    (A) unlike most of his predecessors
    (B) unlike most of their predecessors
    (C) unlike previous inventors
    (D) whereas their predecessors
    (E) the opposite of previous robots

18. After hearing the inspiring presentation given by the county fire chief, each person attending the meeting decided <u>they would be a volunteer firefighter</u>.

    (A) they would be a volunteer firefighter
    (B) they will become volunteer firefighters
    (C) to become a volunteer firefighter
    (D) to become volunteer firefighters
    (E) to be volunteer firefighters

19. The cat's habit of scratching vertical objects helps them not only to keep their claws sharp but also to mark its territory.

    (A) The cat's habit of scratching vertical objects helps them not only to keep their
    (B) The cat's habit of scratching vertical objects helps it to keep its
    (C) The habit of scratching vertical objects helps the cat to not only keep its
    (D) Their habit of scratching vertical objects helps the feline only to keep their
    (E) The feline habit to scratch vertical objects helps them not only to keep their

20. Although it was <u>proven long ago</u> that common colds are caused <u>only by</u> viruses, many people
                       A   B

    <u>persist in</u> the erroneous belief that <u>it can be</u> contracted through mere exposure to cold air.
       C   D

    <u>No error</u>
    E

2-B. Unclear pronoun reference

In some sentences, the problem is that it isn't clear what word the pronoun refers to.

Example: Alice, Bethany, and Colleen were having lunch when she remembered a previous appointment.

Who remembered the appointment? It isn't clear who "she" refers to. When you see a pronoun whose antecedent isn't obvious, ask yourself who or what the pronoun refers to. If the answer isn't clear, then there is an unclear pronoun reference.

Exercise set 2-B: Unclear pronoun reference

Choose the answer that results in a clear and concise sentence, free from awkwardness or ambiguity.

1. Because the stained-glass windows of a large basilica in Paris were destroyed during World War I, it encouraged extensive removal of stained-glass windows from cathedrals throughout France during the World War II.

    (A) War I, it encouraged
    (B) War I, they encouraged
    (C) War I; then there was
    (D) War I, there was
    (E) War I, encouraging

2. In African art, which was a primary source of inspiration for Swedish sculptor Carl Milles, it offered a wealth of forms, shapes, colors, and patterns.

 (A) In African art, which was a primary source of inspiration for Swedish sculptor Carl Milles, it offered a wealth of forms, shapes, colors, and patterns.
 (B) In African art, a primary source of inspiration, offering Swedish sculptor Carl Milles a wealth of forms, shapes, colors, and patterns.
 (C) African art, for Swedish sculptor Carl Milles, offered him a primary source of inspiration, a wealth of forms, shapes, colors, and patterns.
 (D) African art, with its wealth of forms, shapes, colors, and patterns, offering Swedish sculptor Carl Milles a primary source of inspiration.
 (E) For Swedish sculptor Carl Milles, African art was a primary source of inspiration, offering a wealth of forms, shapes, colors, and patterns.

3. In 1963, Betty Friedan published *The Feminine Mystique*, in which it analyzed the happiness of women in terms of education and careers.

 (A) *The Feminine Mystique*, in which it analyzed the happiness
 (B) *The Feminine Mystique* where it analyzed the happiness
 (C) *The Feminine Mystique,* which analyzed the happiness
 (D) *The Feminine Mystique*, it analyzed the happiness
 (E) *The Feminine Mystique*, women's happiness was analyzed

4. Fossils are of great interest to archaeologists and anthropologists, since this is how they obtain information about early civilizations.

 (A) to archaeologists and anthropologists, since this is how they obtain information
 (B) to archaeologists and anthropologists, who obtain from them information
 (C) to archaeologists and anthropologists because information is obtained by them
 (D) to archaeologists and anthropologists; they obtain information this way
 (E) to archaeologists and anthropologists, which is how they obtain information

5. Scientists have recently learned that not all genes behave according to Mendel's predicted
                    A
 patterns of inheritance; it has forced them to reexamine some previously unquestionable
                           B   C   D
 assumptions. No error
              E

SAT Grammar—Prioritized   37

6. To fulfill a school assignment, Tiffany, Mariah, and Kathleen were each writing a critique of twenty art pieces; the curator asked her if she needed help.

   (A) the curator asked her if she needed help
   (B) the curator asked her if they needed help
   (C) the curator asked them if she needed help
   (D) the curator asks her if she needed help
   (E) the curator asked them if they needed help

7. In the championship game, they had to end the contest early because of threatening weather.

   (A) they had to end the contest early
   (B) they must have ended the contest early
   (C) they ended the contest early
   (D) they had ended the contest early
   (E) the officials ended the contest early

8. My sisters have learned a lot by playing in the school orchestra, so I have also chosen it as my extracurricular activity.

   (A) so I have also chosen it
   (B) so I have also chosen music
   (C) so I have elected to choose it
   (D) so I have also chose it
   (E) so I had also chosen it

9. Meteorites are of great interest to scientists, because this is how they obtain information about the presence of various metals in other parts of the solar system.

   (A) scientists, because this is how they obtain information
   (B) scientists, who study them to obtain information
   (C) scientists because information is obtained by them
   (D) scientists; they obtain information this way
   (E) scientists, which is how they obtain information

10. Lucille and Evelyn <u>agree that her son Tyler</u> spends too much time playing video games.

    (A) agree that her son Tyler
    (B) agrees that her son Tyler
    (C) agree that Tyler, her son,
    (D) agree that Evelyn's son Tyler
    (E) agree that her son Tyler, Evelyn's that is,

11. Harrison, Cynthia, and Olivia <u>were hiking</u> <u>when</u> <u>she lost her</u> footing <u>on a steep part</u> of the
                                              A   B   C   D
    path. <u>No error</u>
          E

12. Because Emily wants to reduce the sugar intake in her diet, <u>she avoided prepared foods</u> containing sucrose and fructose.

    (A) she avoided prepared foods
    (B) she avoided having eaten prepared foods
    (C) she avoided foods prepared in such a way that they are
    (D) she avoids prepared foods
    (E) she is avoiding prepared foods

13. Bill <u>invited</u> Eric to <u>his</u> hunting camp for the weekend <u>because</u> <u>he</u> enjoyed being outdoors.
            A   B   C   D
    <u>No error</u>
      E

14. After Sarah and Teresa visited Yellowstone National Park, <u>she said she should have taken more pictures</u>.

    (A) she said she should have taken more pictures
    (B) Sarah said she should have taken more pictures
    (C) Sarah says she should have taken more pictures
    (D) she said Sarah should have taken more pictures
    (E) she said they should have taken more pictures

15. When Wilson and Sierra met Jackson at the mall, he asked if they wanted to join him in the food court to get something to eat.

    (A) he asked if they wanted to join him in the food court to get something to eat
    (B) he asked both of them if they wanted to go to the food court to get something to eat
    (C) he asked if they wanted to go with him to eat at the food court
    (D) Jackson asked if they wanted to join him at the food court
    (E) Jackson asked if they were wanting to go to the food court to get something to eat

16. Soon after the city council voted in favor of the new dog park, Steve and Jason agreed that he would to be the first one to take his dog there.

    (A) Steve and Jason agreed that he would to be the first one to take his dog there
    (B) Steve and Jason agreed that Jason would to be the first one taking his dog there
    (C) Steve and Jason agreed that they would to be the first ones to take their dog there
    (D) Steve and Jason agreed that they would to be the first one to take their dog there
    (E) Steve and Jason agreed that he would to be the first one to take Steve's dog there

17. Brenda, Jessie, and Michael were hiking when, stumbling over a tree root, he fell down a steep embankment.

    (A) when, stumbling over a tree root, he fell down
    (B) and then, stumbling over a tree root, he fell down
    (C) when, he fell, stumbling over a tree root, down
    (D) when Michael, stumbling over a tree root, fell down
    (E) when, stumbling over a tree root, Michael had fallen down

18. Political candidates seldom say anything nice about their opponents; their goal, after all, is if you elect them.

    (A) opponents; their goal, after all, is if you elect them
    (B) opponents; the candidates' goal, after all, is if you elect them
    (C) opponents; the candidates' goal, after all, is to get elected
    (D) opponents; after all, the candidates' goal is if you elect them
    (E) opponents; their goals, after all, are if you elect them

19. In the physics textbook my grandfather <u>used</u> in high school, <u>it</u> <u>states</u> that an atom <u>cannot be</u>
                                                   A   B C   D

    split. <u>No error</u>
              E

20. Scientists <u>have recently discovered</u> that not all genes <u>adhere</u> to formerly-accepted theories of
                                 A   B

    inheritance; <u>it has</u> forced <u>them</u> to reexamine some widely-held assumptions. <u>No error</u>
                      C   D   E

2-C. Shift in Point of View

Make sure that a sentence doesn't shift point of view. In other words, if the sentence starts out in second person, using "you," then it should not switch to "one" later on.

Example: In order for *you* to get the most out of *your* GPS, *one* should spend some time reading the manual.

"One" should be "you."

In the following sentences, watch for a shift in point of view.

Exercise set 2-C: Shift in Point of View

Choose the answer that results in a clear and concise sentence, free from awkwardness or ambiguity.

1. If <u>one spends</u> <u>a lot of</u> time with children, you should understand that a promise <u>made to</u> a child
          A   B   C

   is a solemn matter because the child <u>will never</u> forget it. <u>No error</u>
                                                             D   E

2. Health professionals <u>caution that</u> people <u>who are inactive</u> are <u>likely to</u> gain weight, especially
                                         A   B   C

   after <u>you</u> have reached middle age. <u>No error</u>
           D   E

3. When purchasing a house, buyers must consider whether he or she can afford the cost of maintaining the property.

   (A) When purchasing a house, buyers must consider whether he or she can afford the cost of maintaining the property.
   (B) When purchasing a house, the cost of maintaining the property must be considered affordable to buyers.
   (C) When purchasing new houses, buyers must consider whether they can afford the cost of maintaining the property.
   (D) When purchasing new houses, buyers must consider whether the cost of maintaining the property can be afforded by them.
   (E) When a new house is purchased, buyers must consider whether one can afford their the cost of maintaining the property.

4. When picking me up at an airport, Jim must pay close attention to the clearance required for one's camper.

   (A) clearance required for one's camper.
   (B) clearance required for their camper.
   (C) clearance requiring for one's camper.
   (D) clearance one's camper requires.
   (E) clearance required for his camper.

5. Librarians report that the more books people check out, the more likely it is that he or she
                                       A   B   C
   has read classics such as *To Kill a Mockingbird* by Harper Lee. No error
                   D   E

6. Alfredo was spending the week with his dad in Boston, where they were going to watch two
            A   B   C   D
   Celtics games. No error
                   E

7. Achieving the very best is difficult for even the most dedicated student, regardless of whether you are trying to become a better musician, student, or athlete.

   (A) regardless of whether you are
   (B) regardless of whether he is
   (C) regardless of whether or not you are
   (D) no matter if you are
   (E) even if you are

8. The renowned actor Sean Connery was interested in drama because he believed that if you bring historical events alive on stage, it could have a lasting impact.

   (A) if you bring historical events alive on stage, it could have
   (B) if you bring historical events alive on stage, you could have
   (C) if you bring historical events alive on stage, they could have
   (D) by bringing historical events alive on stage has
   (E) bringing historical events alive on stage has

9. Animal keepers have expanded one's definition of care to include concern for the animal's mental needs as well as for its physical needs.

   (A) have expanded one's definition of care to include
   (B) have expanded one's definition of care, including
   (C) expanded their definition of care, they include
   (D) expanding the definition of care to include
   (E) have expanded their definition of care to include

10. As the guide led us through the exhibit of ancient Persian paintings, she interspersed
    A   B
    explanations of the objects with stories about her own first encounter with Persian art,
                                                           C
    giving you a unique personal dimension to the tour. No error
    D   E

11. Its rays shining through the stained glass, the late afternoon sun treated us to their many
                   A   B   C   D
    colorful hues on the pale wall of the chapel. No error
                                                  E

12. Nutrition experts <u>recommend</u> that <u>before making</u> drastic changes to <u>your</u> diet, a person
                                A   B   C
    <u>should consult</u> his physician. <u>No error</u>
           D   E

13. To attract wide audiences, radio stations <u>sequence songs such that listeners to not have to wait too long before hearing a song you like</u>.

    (A) sequence songs such that listeners to not have to wait too long before hearing a song you like
    (B) therefore sequence songs such that listeners to not have to wait too long before hearing a song you like
    (C) sequence songs such that no one has to wait too long before hearing a song you like
    (D) sequences songs such that no one has to wait too long before hearing a song he or she likes
    (E) sequence songs such that listeners to not have to wait too long before hearing a song they like

14. Doctors warn that people who are inactive are more like to have high cholesterol, <u>especially after you have reached middle age</u>.

    (A) especially after you have reached middle age
    (B) especially after middle age has been reached
    (C) especially after they have reached middle age
    (D) especially after you having reached middle age
    (E) especially after one has reached middle age

15. The movie critic <u>crafted</u> his review with great diplomacy, <u>attempting</u> <u>to express</u> his disdain of
                               A   B   C
    the movie without offending <u>one's</u> readers. <u>No error</u>
                                        D   E

16. If one wants to become <u>a good speaker, he or she should</u> remember to keep gestures to a minimum.

    (A) a good speaker, he or she should
    (B) good speakers, he or she should
    (C) a good speaker, one should
    (D) a good speaker, they should
    (E) a good speaker, then he or she should

17. Some girls, when shopping for a prom dress, <u>fail</u> to take into <u>consideration</u> <u>the cost</u> of <u>her</u>
                                                                 A   B   C   D

    accessories. <u>No error</u>
                    E

18. Studies show that the longer the line is at an ATM, <u>the less likely that he or she will get out of the line and leave</u>.

    (A) the less likely that he or she will get out of the line and leave
    (B) the less likely that one will get out of the line and leave
    (C) the less likely that they will get out of the line and leave
    (D) the likelihood decreases that he or she will get out of the line and leave
    (E) someone will be less likely to get out of the line and leave

19. Understanding the difference between disagreement and insult <u>is critical if one is to engage in a constructive argument with your peers</u>.

    (A) is critical if one is to engage in a constructive argument with your peers
    (B) are critical if one is to engage in a constructive argument with your peers
    (C) is critical if you are to engage in a constructive argument with your peers
    (D) is critical if one is to engage your peers in a constructive argument
    (E) is critical if he or she is to engage in a constructive argument with your peers

20. Having read all of Lee Child's Jack Reacher novels, <u>Greg concluded that Reacher's code of conduct was similar to his own</u>.

    (A) Greg concluded that Reacher's code of conduct was similar to his own
    (B) Greg concluded that Reacher's code of conduct was similar to their own
    (C) Greg concluded that one's own code of conduct was similar to Reacher's
    (D) Greg has concluded that Reacher's code of conduct was similar to his own
    (E) Greg concluded that Reacher's code of conduct was similar to his or her own

2-D. Nominative vs. objective case

Personal pronouns are words that refer to people, such as *he*, *they*, *me*, etc. Personal pronouns are either Nominative or Objective case, depending on the use in the sentence.

A nominative case pronoun is used as the subject, and an objective case pronoun is used as a direct object, an indirect object, or the object of a preposition.

Nominative Case	Objective Case
I	me
you	you
he	him
she	her
we	us
they	them

Nominative Case pronouns are used as the *subject*: I study. You study. He studies. She studies. We study. They study.

Objective Case pronouns are used as the *direct object*: Drive me. Drive you. Drive him. Drive her. Drive us. Drive them.

Objective Case pronouns are used as the *indirect object*: Throw me the ball. Throw you the ball. Throw him the ball. Throw her the ball. Throw us the ball. Throw them the ball.

Objective Case pronouns are used as the *object of a preposition*: Cook for me. Cook for you. Cook for him. Cook for her. Cook for us. Cook for them.

A common error on the test—as well as in real life—occurs when more than one person follows a preposition and the nominative case pronoun is used, such "Jerry asked Bill and I." But we wouldn't say "Jerry asked I." Temporarily remove the other person from the sentence and let your ear be your guide. "Jerry asked me." "Jerry asked Bill." Therefore, it should be "Jerry asked Bill and me."

Exercise set 2-D: Nominative vs. objective case

Choose the answer that results in a clear and concise sentence, free from awkwardness or ambiguity.

1. Although the guest list is <u>limited</u>, <u>for the most part</u>, to a few friends and immediate families,
                                     A   B
   it includes Sandra and <u>I,</u> long-time friends <u>of both</u> the bride and the groom. <u>No error</u>.
                         C   D   E

2. When the prom <u>was</u> only a few weeks away, <u>Terrence and me</u> began to have doubts <u>about</u>
                        A   B   C
   putting so much money and effort <u>into preparing</u> for an event that would last only a few hours.
                                       D
   <u>No error</u>
     E

3. <u>As</u> a revolutionary, Fidel Castro was instrumental in <u>organizing</u> a group of rebels in Cuba, and
     A   B
   it was <u>him</u> who in 1959 <u>overthrew</u> the government of Gen. Fulgencio Batista. <u>No error</u>
         C   D   E

4. Although Justin normally was not <u>one</u> to volunteer, Barbara and <u>him</u> spent all day Saturday
                                          A   B
   <u>helping</u> out <u>at</u> the soup kitchen. <u>No error</u>
     C   D   E

5. My grandmother, <u>whose</u> advice I have always <u>followed</u>, knows my abilities and <u>weaknesses</u>
                       A   B   C
   better than <u>myself</u>. <u>No error</u>
              D   E

6. Unwilling to delay the verdict any longer, <u>the other</u> jurors and <u>me</u>, deadlocked <u>throughout</u> the
                                         A   B   D
   deliberations, now <u>worked to</u> resolve our disparate opinions. <u>No error</u>
                           D   E

7. <u>Born in</u> Puerto Rico, actress Isabella Cortes became so renowned in Mexico <u>during</u> the 1940s
     A   B
   <u>that film</u> companies rushed to make movies featuring <u>she</u> and her husband, Alejandro Cortes.
     C   D
   <u>No error</u>
     E

8. <u>Those</u> <u>who</u> challenged <u>the right of</u> Parliament to impose taxes on the colonies thought the
     A   B   C
   tobacco tax was just as offensive <u>to them as</u> the tea tax. <u>No error</u>
                                     D   E

9. Last month, when Divya's aunt and uncle <u>came from</u> India to visit their relatives <u>and tour</u> the
                                                  A   B
   United States, Divya invited <u>Pauline and I</u> to her house <u>to meet</u> them. <u>No error</u>
                                      C   D   E

10. Our new employee, who shares several interests with me, asked to join Carol and I on our next marathon trip.

    (A) who shares several interests with me, asked to join Carol and I
    (B) whom shares several interests with me, asked to join Carol and I
    (C) who shares several of my interests with me, asked to join Carol and I
    (D) who shares several interests with me, asked to join Carol and me
    (E) who is sharing several interests with me, asked to join Carol and I

11. Galileo used a telescope to study the moon and Venus; it was him who first saw the four
            A   B   C   D
    large moons of Jupiter. No error
                            E

12. Between you and I, I don't agree with the principal's decision.

    (A) Between you and I
    (B) Among you and I
    (C) Between I and you
    (D) Between you or I
    (E) Between you and me

13. In his novel, *Learning Against Their Will*, Donald Laurence presents a fictionalized account of both he and his sister's experiences as teachers in inner city schools.

    (A) of both he and his sister's experiences as teachers
    (B) of both his and his sister's experiences as teachers
    (C) of the experiences as teachers of both he and his sister
    (D) of both him and his sister's experiences as teachers
    (E) of their experiences as teachers

14. When my brother Daniel and I had broken legs at the same time, our mother had to drive him and I to school.

    (A) our mother had to drive him and I to school
    (B) our mother had to drive he and I to school
    (C) our mother had to drive him and me to school
    (D) to get him and I to school, our mother had to drive
    (E) our mother had driven him and me to school

15. When our teacher selected Joanne and I to represent our school at the state's mock government day, we were so excited that we jumped out of our chairs.

    (A) When our teacher selected Joanne and I to represent our school
    (B) When our teacher selected Joanne and I to be representing our school
    (C) When our teacher selected Joanne, as well as me, to represent our school
    (D) When our teacher selected me and Joanne to represent our school
    (E) When our teacher selected Joanne and me to represent our school

16. In her autobiography, Emily Smith Houston, who was a close friend of fellow novelist Charles Underwood, included her observations of he and several other contemporary writers.

    (A) included her observations of he and several other
    (B) included her observations on he and several other
    (C) included her observations of himself and several other
    (D) included her observations of him and several other
    (E) included her observations of both he and several other

17. The interviewer asked Michelle and I if we would like to appear in a documentary about marathons.

    (A) The interviewer asked Michelle and I if we would like to appear
    (B) The interviewer asked Michelle and I to appear, if we would like to,
    (C) The interviewer asked Michelle and I if we would like to be appearing
    (D) The interviewer asked Michelle and myself if we would like to appear
    (E) The interviewer asked Michelle and me if we would like to appear

18. After being nominated for the prestigious award, the young actress predicted that the award would go to either Susan Westerling or her.

    (A) the award would go to either Susan Westerling or her
    (B) the award would go to either Susan Westerling or she
    (C) the award would be going to either Susan Westerling or her
    (D) the award would go to one or the other of Susan Westerling or her
    (E) the award would go to either Susan Westerling or to she

19. Mrs. Spencer, impressed with Maria's science project, <u>invited she and Allison to attend</u> the state-wide science competition in May.

    (A) invited she and Allison to attend
    (B) invited her and Allison to attend
    (C) invited she and her friend Allison to attend
    (D) invited she and Allison to be attending
    (E) has invited she and Allison to attend

20. Because he wanted more girls at his graduation party, Jacob <u>asked Jessica and I to bring</u> as many of our friends as we wanted.

    (A) asked Jessica and I to bring
    (B) asked Jessica, along with me, to bring
    (C) asked Jessica and me if we could be bringing
    (D) asked Jessica and me to bring
    (E) asked Jessica and I about bring

2-E. Unnecessary pronoun or no antecedent

Some sentences contain a pronoun that isn't needed, or one that has no antecedent. For example, some sentences contain *they* without a word for *they* to refer to.

Example: Because the tree roots are causing the pavement on my street to buckle, they should remove the tree.

Who should remove the tree? We don't know.
In other sentences, a pronoun is used unnecessarily.

Example: The members of the debate team, *they* placed second overall at a recent statewide competition.

In this case, *they* isn't needed and should be removed.

Correct: The members of the debate team placed second overall at a recent statewide competition.

Exercise set 2-E: Unnecessary pronoun or no antecedent

Choose the answer that results in a clear and concise sentence, free from awkwardness or ambiguity.

1. Because of the prices they bring, tuna have been overfished; some North Atlantic breeding populations <u>they estimate to decline</u> by about 90 percent since 1980.

    (A) they estimate to decline
    (B) they estimated to have declined
    (C) it is estimated that they have declined
    (D) are estimated to decline
    (E) are estimated to have declined

2. <u>Dr. Edwin Morrison's revolutionary research in industrial medicine resulted in them uncovering many health risks in the workplace.</u>

    (A) Dr. Edwin Morrison's revolutionary research in industrial medicine resulted in them uncovering many health risks in the workplace.
    (B) Dr. Edwin Morrison's revolutionary research in industrial medicine led to the uncovering of
    many health risks in the workplace.
    (C) They exposed many health risks in the workplace and it was because of the result of Dr. Edwin Morrison's revolutionary research.
    (D) Industrial medicine research, revolutionized by Dr. Edwin Morrison, resulted in their uncovering of many health risks in the workplace.
    (E) Dr. Edwin Morrison revolutionized industrial medicine research, which is why many health risks in the workplace were uncovered.

3. The responsibility of a part-time job can be a great benefit to a student; <u>all of them must learn</u> time management in order to succeed in college or the workplace.

    (A) all of them must learn
    (B) all of them are learning
    (C) all of whom must learn
    (D) they have to learn
    (E) he or she must learn

4. Centuries ago, the Phoenician emphasis on exploration and trade caused it to earn the admiration and envy of other peoples.

   (A) the Phoenician emphasis on exploration and trade cause it to earn
   (B) by emphasizing exploration and trade, this caused the Phoenicians to earn
   (C) Phoenician emphasis on exploration and trade caused them to earn
   (D) an emphasis on exploration and one on trade led to the Phoenician's earning
   (E) an emphasis on exploration and trade earned the Phoenicians

5. Even after railroads were becoming more widespread, you couldn't take them across the country.

   (A) you couldn't take them
   (B) you couldn't take it
   (C) they couldn't be taken
   (D) they couldn't take them
   (E) it couldn't be taken

6. My advisor suggested I try either French or Spanish for my foreign language, but you won't know what you like until you've tried it.

   (A) but you won't know what you like until you've tried it
   (B) but we won't know what we like until we've tried it
   (C) but they won't know what they like until they've tried it
   (D) but I won't know what I like before the point I try it
   (E) but I won't know what I like until I've tried it

7. During the blackout last week, Veronica, like everyone else, she coped in the best way she could.

   (A) Veronica, like everyone else, she coped in the best way she could
   (B) Veronica, like everyone else, coped in the best way she could
   (C) Veronica, like everyone else, she coped in the best way they could
   (D) Veronica, like everyone else, was coping in the best way they could
   (E) Veronica, like everyone else, coped in the best way they could

8. By them feeding on dead animals, the bald eagle is one of many animals that plays a crucial role in nature's recycling process.

    (A) By them feeding
    (B) By their feeding
    (C) By feeding
    (D) They feed
    (E) It feeds

9. Carolyn Curiel, who crafted many of President Bill Clinton's speeches, she also served as ambassador to Belize from 1997 to 2001.

    (A) speeches, she also served
    (B) speeches, also served
    (C) speeches, and served
    (D) speeches as well as serving
    (E) speeches and served

10. By engaging in vigorous exercise for a minimum of 30 minutes every day, it can lower levels of bad cholesterol by as much as one third.

    (A) By engaging in vigorous exercise for a minimum of 30 minutes every day, it
    (B) If one engages in vigorous exercise for a minimum of 30 minutes every day, it
    (C) If you engage in vigorous exercise for a minimum of 30 minutes every day, one
    (D) Engaging in vigorous exercise for a minimum of 30 minutes every day
    (E) To engage in vigorous exercise for a minimum of 30 minutes every day, it

11. In a recent SAT class, several students, they asked very good questions about grammar and usage.

    (A) several students, they asked
    (B) several students are asking
    (C) several students were asking
    (D) several students asked
    (E) several students had asked

12. If you live in the New York City area, you probably know that they broadcast the New York City Marathon live on several local television stations.

    (A) that they broadcast the New York City Marathon live
    (B) that the New York City Marathon is broadcast live
    (C) that they live broadcast the New York City Marathon
    (D) which the New York City Marathon is broadcast live
    (E) that it is broadcast live

13. In 2010, after the New Orleans Saints won Superbowl XLIV, they celebrated in the streets of New Orleans all night.

    (A) they celebrated in the streets
    (B) they were celebrated in the streets
    (C) fans celebrated in the streets
    (D) they have celebrated in the streets
    (E) they were celebrating in the streets

14. Soon after hearing about the robbery at my neighborhood pharmacy, I knew they would find the perpetrator or perpetrators soon.

    (A) I knew they would find
    (B) I knew he or she would find
    (C) I have known they would find
    (D) I knew they will find
    (E) I knew the police would find

15. Because the potholes on my street keep growing larger each month, I hope they come to fix them soon.

    (A) I hope they come to fix them soon
    (B) I hope they come to fix them sooner
    (C) I hope they will come to fix them soon
    (D) I hope the county comes to fix them soon
    (E) I hope they are coming to fix them soon

16. When I went to city hall to ask about getting a permit for a road race, they told me it would cost twenty-five dollars.

    (A) they told me it would cost
    (B) I was told it would cost
    (C) they told me it would be costing
    (D) she told me it would cost
    (E) they said that it would cost

17. The group of bystanders stood looking at the wreckage of the three cars, they were saying how suddenly the collision occurred.

    (A) cars, they were saying how suddenly
    (B) cars, they had been saying how suddenly
    (C) cars, saying how suddenly
    (D) cars, they said how suddenly
    (E) cars, were saying how suddenly

18. Since my daughter was so proud of her first bicycle, and had decorated it with streamers and a bell, I'm surprised I had forgotten it.

    (A) I'm surprised I had forgotten it
    (B) I'm surprised I had forgotten her
    (C) I'm surprised I forgot about it
    (D) I'm surprised I had forgotten the bike
    (E) I'm surprised I had been forgetting all about it

19. In all the excitement of my surprise party, it was not until afterward that I wondered how they had planned it without me finding out about it.

    (A) it was not until afterward that I wondered how they had planned it
    (B) I didn't wonder until afterward how it had been planned
    (C) it was not until afterward that I had wondered how they planned it
    (D) not until afterward did I wonder how it had been planned by them
    (E) it was not until afterward that I was wondering how the party had been planned

20. The seniors <u>they should have completed</u> all the requirements for graduation by Wednesday, May 28.

   (A) they should have completed
   (B) they should be completing
   (C) they will be completing
   (D) should have completed
   (E) who should have completed

2-F: Relative pronouns

Relative pronouns introduce a dependent clause that modifies a noun (person or thing). Keep in mind the meaning of the pronoun. For example, it is incorrect to say, ". . .the museum when. . ." because the museum isn't a time. *Who* and *whom* refer to people, *which* and *that* refer to a thing or things, *when* and *while* refer to time, *there* and *where* refer to a place, etc.

Exercise set 2-F: Relative pronouns: who, whom, which, that, when, while, etc.

Choose the answer that results in a clear and concise sentence, free from awkwardness or ambiguity.

1. Enrico Fermi immigrated from Italy to the United States at a time in history <u>where governments in Europe were growing unstable</u>.

   (A) where governments in Europe were growing unstable
   (B) where governments in Europe grow unstable
   (C) where governments in Europe had grown unstable
   (D) when governments in Europe were growing unstable
   (E) where governments in Europe will be growing unstable

2. Because we knew that koalas get a plentiful quantity of water from the eucalyptus leaves they eat, <u>there was no surprise to learn</u> that "koala" is an Aboriginal word that means "no drink animal."

   (A) there was no surprise to learn
   (B) it is no surprise for us in learning
   (C) we were not surprised to learn
   (D) nor surprisingly we learned
   (E) no surprise came to us when we learned

3. Workers <u>which work</u> no more than <u>forty- hour weeks</u> in factories <u>should have</u> more leisure
             A   B   C
   time than those who <u>work demanding</u>, salaried jobs. <u>No error</u>
                            D   E

4. <u>In 1991, while the New Orleans Saints won its</u> first division championship, the fans stopped wearing paper bags on their heads.

   (A) In 1991, while the New Orleans Saints won its
   (B) In 1991, while the New Orleans Saints won its
   (C) In 1991, when the New Orleans Saints had won their
   (D) In 1991, when the New Orleans Saints won its
   (E) In 1991, a time when the New Orleans Saints won its

5. I am deeply indebted to my high school principal, Mr. Loomis, <u>that showed he cared about each student</u> and did everything he could to instill in us the values that would lead to success.

   (A) that showed he cared about each student
   (B) that showed he had concern for each student
   (C) who showed he cared about each student
   (D) which showed he cared about each student
   (E) that showed he cared about each one

6. <u>The race director, responded quickly, made arrangements</u> for an alternate start to the marathon to meet the needs of a small group of runners.

   (A) The race director, responded quickly, made arrangements
   (B) The race director, responded quickly, make arrangements
   (C) The race director, which responded quickly, made arrangements
   (D) The race director, while responding quickly, made arrangements
   (E) The race director, who responded quickly, made arrangements

7. W. E. B. Du Bois, in addition to co-establishing the NAACP and editing its magazine *Crisis*, <u>established a journal call Phylon, who has recently resumed publication</u>.

   (A) established a journal call *Phylon*, who has recently resumed publication
   (B) established a journal call *Phylon*, which has recently resumed publication
   (C) established a journal call *Phylon*, who had recently resumed publication
   (D) established a journal call *Phylon*, recently resumed publication
   (E) established a journal call *Phylon*, who has recently resumed publishing

8. The Anasazi people, which occupied the Mesa Verde region of the Southwestern United States, created entire villages in the sides of cliffs.

    (A) people, which occupied the Mesa Verde region
    (B) people, who occupied the Mesa Verde region
    (C) people, while they occupied the Mesa Verde region
    (D) people, when they occupied the Mesa Verde region
    (E) people, which occupied the Mesa Verde region

9. Most of these cliff dwellings were created between 600 A.D. and 1300 A.D., where the
        A   B   C   D
   Anasazi lived in Utah, Colorado, and New Mexico. No error
                                                         E

10. The dwellings of the Anasazi encompassed a region of nearly 10,000 square miles
                         A   B
    and now form the Mesa Verde National Park. No error
      C   D   E

11. Few people today realize that the Republican Party was originally organized to fight slavery and fought for the Civil Rights Act of 1866, while established African Americans as American citizens and forbade discrimination against them.

    (A) 1866, while established African Americans
    (B) 1866, when established African Americans
    (C) 1866, while it established African Americans
    (D) 1866, while establishing African Americans
    (E) 1866, which established African Americans

12. When the news spread how new goldfields were discovered in the Sacramento area, hundreds flocked to California expecting to become wealthy.

    (A) spread how new goldfields were discovered
    (B) spread how new goldfields had been discovered
    (C) spread about new goldfields
    (D) spread about new goldfields being discovered
    (E) spread that new goldfields were discovered

13. Even though she had published two novels earlier, when Doris Lessing published *The Golden Notebook* in 1962, it instantly established herself as one of the most important literary voices of her generation.

    (A) 1962, it instantly established herself
    (B) 1962, she instantly established herself
    (C) 1962, it had instantly established herself
    (D) 1962, they instantly established herself
    (E) 1962, that instantly established herself

14. Global warming, what play a big role in the melting of tropical glaciers like those in the Peruvian Andes, may cause serious lack of water supply to crops and animals within 20 years.

    (A) warming, what play a big role in the melting of tropical glaciers
    (B) warming, which plays a big role in the melting of tropical glaciers
    (C) warming, what played a big role in the melting of tropical glaciers
    (D) warming, what plays a biggest role in the melting of tropical glaciers
    (E) warming, who play a big role in the melting of tropical glaciers

15. During rehearsals, the director praised the performers which had supporting roles more often
                                          A   B   C
    than those who had the more demanding roles. No error
                    D   E

16. There is a special relationship between a band director and the players, when at its best can be creative and at its worst, demoralizing.

    (A) players, when at its best can be creative
    (B) players, while at its best can be creative
    (C) players, which at its best can be creative
    (D) players, then at its best can be creative
    (E) players, at its best can be creative

17. Astonishing discoveries in gene research may lead to revolutionary changes in medical treatment, where it may be possible to create drugs personalized to a patient's genetic makeup.

    (A) treatment, where it may be possible to create
    (B) treatment, in which they can possibly create
    (C) treatment by making it possible to create
    (D) treatment that makes it possible to create
    (E) treatment so that they can create

18. Throughout the history of science there have been periods where ground-breaking scholars questioned customary assumptions and obsolete theories.

    (A) where ground-breaking scholars questioned
    (B) with ground-breaking scholars questioning
    (C) when ground-breaking scholars questioned
    (D) where questioning by ground-breaking scholars was of
    (E) of when ground-breaking scholars questioned

19. The SAT preparation class, while it includes information about the critical reading, math, and writing sections, will meet on nine consecutive Tuesday evenings.

    (A) class, while it includes information
    (B) class, while it include information
    (C) class, which it includes information
    (D) class, which includes information
    (E) class, when it includes information

20. Isaac Newton developed his revolutionary theories at a time in history where ideas about science were rapidly changing.

    (A) where ideas about science were rapidly changing
    (B) where ideas about science were rapidly change
    (C) where ideas about science had rapidly changed
    (D) when ideas about science were rapidly changing
    (E) where ideas about science will be rapidly changing

3. DANGLING OR MISPLACED MODIFIERS

There are three types of errors here:
   a)   an introductory phrase that modifies the wrong word
   b)   a dangling modifier (an introductory phrase that doesn't modify any word in the sentence)
   c)   a prepositional phrase that modifies the wrong word

Descriptive phrases at the beginning of a sentence modify the first noun or pronoun that follows the phrase, nearly always after a comma. Be sure that the phrase modifies the correct noun or pronoun. Also, be sure that prepositional phrases modify the correct word.

a)   Introductory phrase modifies wrong word

Example: To qualify for the scholarship, the rules require a student to perform thirty hours of community service.

In this sentence, *rules* are qualifying for a scholarship.

Correct: To qualify for the scholarship, a student is required to perform thirty hours of community service.

b)   Dangling modifier

Example: Driving down the highway, the music seemed to get louder and louder.

The music was driving? Who was driving? There is no one in the sentence for "driving" to modify. The sentence needs the driver to follow the comma.

Correct: Driving down the highway, Spencer thought the music seemed to get louder and louder.

c)   Prepositional phrase modified wrong word

Example: On a recent trip to Ft. Worth, I saw the famous Stockyards during a run.

I saw the Stockyards while they were running?

Correct: During a recent trip to Ft. Worth, while I was running I saw the famous Stockyards.

Exercise set 3: Dangling or misplaced modifiers

Choose the answer that results in a clear and concise sentence, free from awkwardness or ambiguity.

1. To satisfy her high school's community service requirement, <u>elderly residents of a senior citizens home were visited by Jan</u> three afternoons a week.

    (A) elderly residents of a senior citizens home were visited by Jan
    (B) Jan visited elderly residents of a senior citizens home
    (C) senior citizens home residents were visited by Jan
    (D) Jan's visit to elderly residents of a senior citizens home was made
    (E) visits by Jan to elderly residents of a senior citizens home were

2. <u>In the preface to the book, it explains</u> why the study of economics is indispensable for anyone interested in a career in politics.

    (A) In the preface to the book, it explains
    (B) It explains in the preface to the book
    (C) The preface to the book explains
    (D) It explains, the preface to the book,
    (E) There is an explanation in the preface to the book to

3. <u>Prior to closing an airplane's outer door, federal regulations require that all electronic devices be powered off.</u>

    (A) Prior to closing an airplane's outer door, federal regulations require that all electronic devices be powered off.
    (B) Prior to closing an airplane's outer door by federal regulations, all electronic devices must be powered off.
    (C) Federal regulations require that all electronic devices be powered off before an airplane's outer door can be closed.
    (D) Federal regulations require that all electronic devices be powered off before they close an airplane's outer door.
    (E) Federal regulations require, before they close an airplane's outer door, that electronic devices be powered off.

4. A beautifully written narrative of the author's boyhood in South America, <u>his descriptions of animal life in the plains region are fascinating</u>.

    (A) his descriptions of animal life in the plains region are fascinating
    (B) his description of animal life in the plains region is fascinating
    (C) he fascinatingly describes animal life in the plains region
    (D) the book contains fascinating descriptions of animal life in the plains region
    (E) the book contains descriptions of animal life in the plains region and they are fascinating

5. Burdened with two large suitcases and heavy scuba gear, Dorothy's search for a luggage cart was frantic.

   (A) Dorothy's search for a luggage cart was frantic
   (B) Dorothy searched frantically for a luggage cart
   (C) Dorothy's frantic search was for a luggage cart
   (D) a luggage cart for which Dorothy frantically searched
   (E) a luggage cart was what Dorothy frantically searched for

6. Following the bomb threat at the theme park, the management announced that all guests' backpacks must be kept in lockers while riding attractions.

   (A) that all guests' backpacks must be kept in lockers while riding attractions
   (B) that all guests riding attractions, they must keep their backpacks in a locker
   (C) that all guests must keep their backpacks in lockers while riding attractions
   (D) that, while riding attractions, all backpacks must be kept in guest lockers
   (E) that, while they ride attractions, all their backpacks must be kept in guest lockers

7. The Villa of the Papyri, which holds the honor of being one of the few classical libraries to survive into modern times, is still intact on the top level, when it was unearthed in 1752.

   (A) survive into modern times, is still intact on the top level, when it was unearthed in 1752
   (B) be surviving into modern times, is still intact on the top level, it was unearthed in 1752
   (C) survive into modern times, is still intact on the top level, it was unearthed in 1752
   (D) survive into modern times, was unearthed in 1752 and found to be still intact on the top level
   (E) survive into modern times, was unearthed in 1752, is still intact on the top level

8. Not actually a member of the genus *Piper*, the early explorers gave the chili pepper its name because they believed they had found the plant that produces black pepper.

   (A) Not actually a member of the genus *Piper*, the early explorers gave the chili pepper its name because they believed
   (B) The chili pepper is not actually a member of the genus *Piper*, it earned that name because early explorers believed
   (C) Early explorers gave the chili pepper, and it was not actually a member of the genus *Piper*, that name on the belief
   (D) Not actually a member of the genus *Piper*, the chili pepper earned that name because early explorers believed

(E) The chili pepper, named by early explorers a member of the genus *Piper* as they believed

9. Hearing no objections from the street's residents at the meeting, <u>the town council's vote was in favor of closing off Jernigan Street to cars</u>.

    (A) the town council's vote was in favor of closing off Jernigan Street to cars
    (B) the town council voted to close off Jernigan Street to cars
    (C) a vote in favor of closing Jernigan Street to cars was made by the town council
    (D) approval to close Jernigan Street to cars was voted by the town council
    (E) the town council, voting, favored to close Jernigan Street to cars

10. In 1885, while teaching at the University of Karlsruhe, <u>the discovery of electromagnetic waves by Heinrich Rudolf Hertz, helped to lay</u> the foundation of quantum physics.

    (A) the discovery of electromagnetic waves by Heinrich Rudolf Hertz helped to lay
    (B) the discovery of electromagnetic waves by Heinrich Rudolf Hertz, helping to lay
    (C) the discovery of electromagnetic waves by Heinrich Rudolf Hertz laid
    (D) Heinrich Rudolf Hertz discovered electromagnetic waves that helped to lay
    (E) Heinrich Rudolf Hertz discovered electromagnetic waves, that had helped to lay

11. Constrained by the small quantities available to them for study, <u>the analysis of certain mold spores in the laboratory attempted by scientists is often frustrated</u>.

    (A) the analysis of certain mold spores in the laboratory attempted by scientists is often frustrated
    (B) analyzing certain mold spores in the laboratory, this often frustrates the attempts of scientists
    (C) scientists are often frustrated in their attempts to analyze mold spores in the laboratory
    (D) scientists attempting to analyze certain mold spores, they are often frustrated
    (E) scientists who attempt to analyze certain mold spores in the laboratory often becoming frustrated

12. Not paying attention to her watch, there was not enough time for the teacher to explain clearly the instructions for the lab assignment.

    (A) Not paying attention to her watch, there was not enough time for the teacher
    (B) With not enough time to pay attention to her watch, there was not enough time for the teacher
    (C) Because the teacher didn't pay attention to her watch, there was not enough time for her
    (D) Having failed to pay attention to her watch, there was not enough time for the teacher
    (E) Not paying attention to her watch, the time was too short for the teacher

13. Running alongside the fast-flowing creek, it was obvious there had been heavy rain for the last few days.

    (A) Running alongside the fast-flowing creek, it was obvious
    (B) Running alongside the fast-flowing creek, it was obviously
    (C) Running alongside the fast-flowing creek, it had been obvious
    (D) Running alongside the fast-flowing creek, it was seemingly obvious
    (E) Running alongside the fast-flowing creek, I thought it was obvious

14. Wanting to reach a total of 300 marathons, Louise's schedule included several five-day marathon series.

    (A) 300 marathons, Louise's schedule included several five-day marathon series.
    (B) 300 marathons, Louise's schedule was to include several five-day marathon series.
    (C) 300 marathons, Louise included several five-day marathon series in her schedule.
    (D) 300 marathons, Louise included a schedule containing several five-day marathon series.
    (E) 300 marathons, several five-day marathon series were included in Louise's schedule.

15. Having enjoyed scuba diving trips all over the world, snow skiing was the sport Dorothy switched to.

    (A) Having enjoyed scuba diving trips all over the world, snow skiing was the sport Dorothy switched to.
    (B) Having enjoyed scuba diving trips all over the world, Dorothy switched to the sport of snow skiing.
    (C) Having enjoyed scuba diving trips all over the world, snow skiing was the sport Dorothy was switching to.
    (D) Having enjoyed scuba diving trips all over the world, Dorothy had switched to the sport of snow skiing.
    (E) Having enjoyed scuba diving trips all over the world, Dorothy switched to snow skiing, the sport.

16. While trying to find the meeting room in the hotel, an old friend was who I saw in the hallway.

    (A) an old friend was who I saw in the hallway
    (B) in the hallway I saw an old friend
    (C) an old friend in the hallway was who I saw
    (D) I saw an old friend in the hallway
    (E) an old friend was the one I saw in the hallway

17. Roaring down the track at seventy miles an hour, the stalled car was smashed by the train.

    (A) Roaring down the track at seventy miles an hour, the stalled car was smashed by the train.
    (B) Roaring down the track at seventy miles an hour, the stalled car was being smashed by the train.
    (C) The train, roaring down the track at seventy miles an hour, was smashing the stalled car.
    (D) Roaring down the track at seventy miles an hour, the train smashed the stalled car.
    (E) Roaring down the track at seventy miles an hour, the stalled car it was smashed by the train.

18. I saw the beautiful yards filled with spring flowers strolling down the street.

    (A) I saw the beautiful yards filled with spring flowers strolling down the street.
    (B) I saw the beautiful yards filled with spring flowers that strolled down the street.
    (C) Strolling down the street, I saw the beautiful yards filled with spring flowers.
    (D) I saw the beautiful yards strolling down the street filled with spring flowers.
    (E) I strolled down the street, there were beautiful yards filled with spring flowers.

19. With a sigh of disappointment, the too-expensive dress was returned to the rack.

    (A) With a sigh of disappointment, the too-expensive dress was returned to the rack.
    (B) With a sigh of disappointment, the too-expensive dress was being returned to the rack.
    (C) With my sigh of disappointment, the too-expensive dress was returned to the rack.
    (D) With a sigh of disappointment, the too-expensive dress was returned to the rack by me.
    (E) With a sigh of disappointment, I returned the too-expensive dress to the rack.

20. Vicious smelly creatures with huge tusks, the ship's crew found it difficult to drive the male walruses from the beach.

    (A) the ship's crew found it difficult to drive the male walruses from the beach
    (B) crew on the ship found it difficult to drive the male walruses from the beach
    (C) it was difficult for the ship's crew to drive the male walruses from the beach
    (D) the male walruses were difficult for the ship's crew drive from the beach
    (E) the ship's crew found the male walruses difficult to drive from the beach

4. PARALLELISM

When items are listed in a series, or two items or ideas are compared or contrasted, the construction of the items should be parallel.

Example: I would prefer to drive alone than sharing a car with other people.

This sentence compares *to drive alone* to *sharing a car* ...

Parallel expressions would be *to drive* and *to share*. A better sentence would be:

I would prefer *to drive* alone than *to share* a car with other people.

Exercise set 4: Parallelism

Choose the answer that results in a clear and concise sentence, free from awkwardness or ambiguity.

1. The contrasting wealth of the business owners compared with the poverty of the factory workers triggered a flood of derisive condemnations from journalists and politicians.

    (A) The contrasting wealth of the business owners compared with
    (B) The contrast to the wealth of the business owners with
    (C) The contrast between the wealth of the business owners and
    (D) In contrast from the wealth of the business owners,
    (E) Contrasting the wealth of the business owners,

2. The physicist felt honored to receive the Comstock Prize, not only because the prize was prestigious and the financial award substantial but also he was, at eighteen, the youngest recipient.

    (A) but also he was, at eighteen,
    (B) but also because he was, at eighteen,
    (C) moreover he was, at eighteen,
    (D) and he, at eighteen, was
    (E) as well as being, at eighteen,

3. The proper timing of traffic lights is important <u>for delay prevention, traffic routing, and accidents</u>.

    (A) for delay prevention, traffic routing, and accidents
    (B) for preventing delays, routing traffic, and accidents
    (C) for delay prevention, traffic routing, and to avoid accidents
    (D) for delay prevention, traffic routing, and accident prevention
    (E) to prevent delays, route traffic, and avoiding accidents

4. On the shore of North Carolina's Kill Devil Hills, the solitude of the beach <u>is awesome, beautiful, and it can be exhilarating</u>.

    (A) is awesome, beautiful, and it can be exhilarating
    (B) is awesome, beautiful, also exhilarating
    (C) is awesome, beautiful, and exhilarating
    (D) being awesome and beautiful, and exhilarating to some people
    (E) is awesome, beautiful, and it can exhilarate some people

5. Abraham Lincoln was famous for his speeches, but he had to labor over them in <u>advance, practiced them thoroughly, and keeping</u> notes in case of memory lapses.

    (A) advance, practiced them thoroughly, and keeping
    (B) advance; to practiced them thoroughly as well as kept
    (C) advance, practicing them thoroughly and keeping
    (D) advance: he was practicing them thoroughly and kept
    (E) advance, he practiced them thoroughly, keeping

6. <u>Ignoring</u> her academic advisors <u>who argued</u> that women could not be engineers, Nancy D.
       A   B
    Fitzroy persisted in her studies, <u>has become</u> among the first engineers <u>to work on</u> the heat
                                               C   D
    transfer of nuclear reactor cores. <u>No error</u>
                                              E

7. When given the option of shopping at the large department stores in the mall or having to go to several stores in different shopping centers, Nancy preferred the mall.

   (A) shopping at the large department stores in the mall or having to go to several stores in different shopping centers
   (B) shopping in the mall at the large department stores having to go to several stores in different shopping centers
   (C) shopping at the large department stores in the mall or having shopped in several stores in different shopping centers
   (D) shopping in the large department stores in the mall or shopping in several stores in different shopping centers
   (E) shopping at the large department stores in the mall along with having to go to several stores in different shopping centers

8. When Jennifer found out her father had made liverwurst sandwiches for lunch, she clutched her stomach, claimed that she was feeling nauseous, and excused herself from the table.

   (A) she clutched her stomach, claimed that she was feeling nauseous, and excused herself from the table
   (B) she clutched her stomach, claimed to feel nauseous, and excused herself from the table
   (C) she clutched her stomach, claimed to feel nauseous, and then was excusing herself from the table
   (D) she had clutched her stomach, claimed that she was feeling nauseous, and excused herself from the table
   (E) she clutched her stomach, claimed to be feeling nauseous, and excused herself from the table

9. In preparation for her run, Alicia did tighten her shoelaces, applied sunscreen, and adjusted the volume on her iPod.

   (A) Alicia did tighten her shoelaces, applied sunscreen, and adjusted the volume on her iPod.
   (B) Alicia did the tightening of her shoelaces, applied sunscreen, and adjusted the volume on her iPod.
   (C) Alicia tightened her shoelaces, applying sunscreen, and adjusted the volume on her iPod.
   (D) Alicia tightened her shoelaces, applied sunscreen, and was adjusting the volume on her iPod.
   (E) Alicia tightened her shoelaces, applied sunscreen, and adjusted the volume on her iPod.

10. We <u>searched the car trunk, the pantry, and the garage, but we could not find</u> the jar of pickles that we remember buying.

    (A) searched the car trunk, the pantry, and the garage, but we could not find
    (B) searched the car trunk, the pantry, and the garage, but we were not finding
    (C) searched the car trunk, looked in the pantry, and the garage, but we could not find
    (D) searched the car trunk, the pantry, and rummaging through the garage, but we could not find
    (E) searched the car trunk, the pantry, and looked in the garage, but we could not find

11. <u>In spite of the air conditioner rattling in the window and the loud music being played by his inconsiderate neighbors,</u> Thomas loved the freedom of his first apartment.

    (A) In spite of the air conditioner rattling in the window and the loud music being played by his
    (B) In spite of the air conditioner rattling in the window and the inconsiderate neighbors playing loud music
    (C) In spite of the air conditioner rattling in the window and the neighbors, being inconsiderate, playing loud music
    (D) In spite of the air conditioner rattled in the window and the inconsiderate neighbors playing loud music
    (E) In spite of the air conditioner rattling in the window or the inconsiderate neighbors playing loud music

12. Not only did Melinda <u>squeal at the sight of the beautiful bouquet, but she also was tearing open the box and eating chocolates</u> all the way to the restaurant.

    (A) squeal at the sight of the beautiful bouquet, but she also was tearing open the box and eating chocolates
    (B) squeal at the sight of the beautiful bouquet, but was tearing open the box and eating chocolates
    (C) squeal at the sight of the beautiful bouquet, but she also tore open the box and ate chocolates
    (D) squeal at the sight of the beautiful bouquet, but she also was tearing the box of chocolates open and eating them
    (E) start squealing at the sight of the beautiful bouquet, but she also tore open the box and eating chocolates

13. Larissa will either add a flock of plastic pink flamingos or she will purchase a family of ceramic gnomes for the front lawn.

    (A) add a flock of plastic pink flamingos or she will purchase a family of ceramic gnomes for
    (B) add a flock of plastic pink flamingos or purchase a family of ceramic gnomes for
    (C) add a flock of plastic pink flamingos or a family of ceramic gnomes to
    (D) add a flock of plastic pink flamingos and she will purchase a family of ceramic gnomes for
    (E) add a flock of plastic pink flamingos or she will have purchased a family of ceramic gnomes for

14. Sandra would rather park three blocks away in the supervised parking building than parking on the street in front of the doctor's office.

    (A) park three blocks away in the supervised parking building than parking on the street
    (B) park three blocks away in the supervised parking building than park on the street
    (C) park three blocks away in the supervised parking building than to be parking on the street
    (D) park three blocks away in the supervised parking building or park on the street
    (E) park three blocks away in the supervised parking building than her park on the street

15. Her ambition was both to serve in the Peace Corps and writing a book about her experiences.

    (A) to serve in the Peace Corps and writing a book about her experiences
    (B) to serve in the Peace Corps and she would write a book about her experiences
    (C) to serve in the Peace Corps and to write a book about her experiences
    (D) to serve in the Peace Corps and to be writing a book about her experiences
    (E) to serve in the Peace Corps and also writing a book about her experiences

16. Either tell me what's on your mind or I wish you would go back to your office.

    (A) Either tell me what's on your mind or I wish you would go back to your office.
    (B) Either tell me what's on your mind or you should go back to your office.
    (C) Either tell me what's on your mind or I am wishing you would go back to your office.
    (D) Either tell me what's on your mind or go back to your office.
    (E) Either tell me what's on your mind or to go back to your office.

17. Mopping the floors and to dust the furniture are two household chores I especially dislike.

    (A) Mopping the floors and to dust the furniture
    (B) Mopping the floors and having to dust the furniture
    (C) Mopping the floors and dusted the furniture
    (D) Mopping the floors or to dust the furniture
    (E) Mopping the floors and dusting the furniture

18. The selection at the downtown CD store is better than going to the mall.

    (A) at the downtown CD store is better than going to the mall
    (B) at the downtown CD store is better than seeing the selection at the mall
    (C) at the downtown CD store is better than theirs at the mall
    (D) at the downtown CD store is better than the one being at the mall
    (E) at the downtown CD store is better than that at the mall

19. The advertisement claims that this toothpaste kills more germs and prevents more cavities than any other toothpaste.

    (A) kills more germs and prevents more cavities
    (B) kills more germs and is preventing more cavities
    (C) kills more germs and prevents the most cavities
    (D) kills more germs and will prevent more cavities
    (E) killed more germs and prevents more cavities

20. My mother made ice cream for my birthday and had asked my brother to try it.

    (A) made ice cream for my birthday and had asked my brother to try it
    (B) made ice cream for my birthday and she had asked my brother to try it
    (C) made ice cream for my birthday and asked my brother to try it
    (D) made ice cream for my birthday and was asking my brother to try it
    (E) made ice cream for my birthday and then had asked my brother to try it

5. WORDY, AWKWARD, OR ILLOGICAL CONSTRUCTION

Some sentences are either wordy or have awkward or illogical construction. Sometimes a word is missing, or an extra word is added. Sentences in this category can fall into three groups:
- a) Missing words, awkward construction
- b) Extra words, redundancies
- c) Poor logic, wrong meaning

a) Missing words, awkward construction

Example: Ben Affleck is both an actor and a director, and this results in his thorough understanding of movie making.

This sentence falls under awkward and wordy construction. First, it isn't clear what "this" is. Second, "this results in" sounds awkward and wordy. A better construction is:

Better: Because Ben Affleck is both an actor and a director, he has a thorough understanding of movie making.

b) Extra words, redundancies

Example: One of the products whose cost has increased greatly in recent years is that of gasoline,

which is more expensive than formerly.

This is wordy. It isn't necessary to say that gasoline "is more expensive than formerly." The sentence already says that the cost has increased, so the "which" clause can be omitted.

Better: One of the products whose cost has increased greatly in recent years is that of gasoline.

c) Poor logic, wrong meaning

Example: Having worked there for most of her adult life, my sister Grace is at a local bakery.

The meaning of this sentence isn't clear. Does it mean that Grace is currently at the local bakery, or does it mean that Grace works at a local bakery. The sentence is neither logical nor clear.

Better: My sister Grace has worked at a local bakery for most of her adult life.

Exercise set 5: Wordy, awkward, or illogical construction

Choose the answer that results in a clear and concise sentence, free from awkwardness or ambiguity.

1. When, in the 1880s, scientists developed the first cultivated blueberry, they lasted longer than the native New Jersey berry and could be sent more markets.

    (A) they lasted longer than the native New Jersey berry and could be sent more markets.
    (B) they could be sent to more markets than the native New Jersey berry because they lasted longer.
    (C) being that they lasted longer than the native New Jersey berry, they could be sent more markets.
    (D) they found them to last longer than the native New Jersey berry. they could be sent more markets.
    (E) they found that it lasted longer than the native New Jersey berry and could be sent more markets.

2. These days, business and social life are conducted at a pace that prompts people to post on social media or send text messages to colleagues and friends rather than phone calls and letters.

    (A) rather than phone calls and letters
    (B) instead of phone calls and letters
    (C) rather than make phone calls or write letters
    (D) instead of to write letters and make phone calls
    (E) rather than making phone calls and writing letters

3. One of the services whose cost has increased greatly in recent years is that of hospital care, which is more expensive than formerly.

    (A) that of hospital care, which is more expensive than formerly
    (B) hospital care which is more expensive than before
    (C) the price of hospital care
    (D) that of hospital care
    (E) hospital care

4. In 2005 Ted Kooser, a former insurance executive, won a Pulitzer Prize for his fourteenth book,
     A B
    Delights and Shadows, a collection of poems focuses on his experiences on the Great Plains.
     C D

    No error.
    E

5. Margaret has learned more about Anne Lamott's writings than the rest of us because of being her favorite author.

    (A) us because of being her favorite author
    (B) us; this is the result of Lamott's being her favorite author
    (C) us because Lamott is her favorite author
    (D) us as a result of Lamott being her favorite author
    (E) us since Lamott is her favorite as an author

6. John Coltrane, a soul jazz saxophonist, often departed from its aesthetic tradition when collaborating with experimental jazz musicians.

    (A) often departed from its aesthetic tradition when collaborating
    (B) he often departs from its aesthetic tradition when collaborating
    (C) collaborates, often departing from the aesthetic traditions of soul jazz
    (D) when he collaborated, often departs from the aesthetic traditions of soul jazz
    (E) often departed from the aesthetic traditions of soul jazz when he collaborated

7. The economy languished through a recession that was as deep, if not deeper than, the
     A B
    recession that had developed four decades earlier. No error.
     C D E

8. After we consulted with the elderly care foundation, they found a place for which she could afford.

    (A) foundation, they found a place for which she
    (B) foundation, they found a place for she
    (C) foundation, they found a place for that she
    (D) foundation, they found a place she
    (E) foundation, they found her a place for which she

9. Dennis Webber was both an engineer and a mathematician, and this resulted in his intimate understanding of the missile project.

    (A) Dennis Webber was both an engineer and a mathematician, and this resulted in his
    (B) Because he was both an engineer and a mathematician, Dennis Webber had an
    (C) That Dennis Webber was both an engineer and a mathematician was why he had an
    (D) The result of this being an engineer and a mathematician was for Dennis Webber to have an
    (E) Dennis Webber was both an engineer and a mathematician, he had an

10. By encouraging young children to save a portion of their allowance will likely enhance the children's ability to manage their money when they become adults.

    (A) By encouraging young children to save a portion of their allowance
    (B) Encouraging young children to save a portion of their allowance
    (C) If young children are encouraged to save a portion of their allowance
    (D) Young children who are encouraged to save a portion of their allowance
    (E) Because they encourage young children to save a portion of their allowance

11. For any viewpoint or opinion, there is always an opposite viewpoint or opinion that disagrees with it.

    (A) there is always an opposite viewpoint or opinion that disagrees with it
    (B) there is always an opposite viewpoint or opinion that disagrees
    (C) an opposite viewpoint or opinion is always there
    (D) there is always an opposite viewpoint or opinion
    (E) opposite viewpoints and opinions always disagree with it

12. John G. Neihardt wanted to bring the story and spirituality of the Sioux holy man Black Elk to the larger world, having accomplished this in his book *Black Elk Speaks*.

    (A) world, having accomplished this
    (B) world and also to accomplish this
    (C) world, that accomplishment is what he did
    (D) world and eventually did it
    (E) world, and he eventually did so

13. Even though Rosalind's public writing <u>may seem</u> pompous, her private writing <u>appears</u> relaxed
    ————————————————————————————————A——————————————————————————————————————B
    and eloquent, <u>as in</u> the letters to her husband concerning her <u>being working</u> in public relations.
    ——————————————C——D
    <u>No error</u>
    E

14. The ribbon shirt, <u>often worn</u> throughout the southwestern United States on special occasions,
    ——————————————A
    <u>was derived</u> from a style <u>imported by settlers</u> and <u>adapted by</u> Native Americans in the early
    ——B————————————————C————————————————D
    1900s. <u>No error</u>
    ————————E

15. Because beavers' teeth never stop growing, <u>there is no surprise to learn</u> that they must constantly gnaw on objects to keep them at a manageable length.

    (A) there is no surprise to learn
    (B) it is no surprise for us in learning
    (C) we were not surprised to learn
    (D) not surprisingly we learned
    (E) no surprise came to us learning

16. Emotional awareness programs <u>teach children and adults how to listen, think critically, and problem solving</u>—skills necessary for getting along with others.

    (A) teach children and adults how to listen, think critically, and problem solving
    (B) teach children and adults how to listen, think critically, and solve problems
    (C) that teach children and adults how to listen, think critically, and problem solving
    (D) teach children and adults listening, to think critically, and solve problems
    (E) teaching children and adults how to listen, thinking critically, and problem solving

17. The struggling performing arts center may have to shut down soon because most of its money has been spent and <u>there is an insufficiency of new revenue coming in</u> to pay expenses.

    (A) there is an insufficiency of new revenue coming in
    (B) insufficienct new revenue coming
    (C) an insufficiency of revenue
    (D) its revenue is insufficient there
    (E) its revenue is insufficient

18. Increasingly aware of the mosquito's role in transmitting West Nile virus, and fearing of an epidemic, the governor finally decided to issue an order to spray all lakes in the state.

    (A) virus, and fearing of an epidemic,
    (B) virus and because of being fearing about an epidemic,
    (C) virus, and fearful of an epidemic,
    (D) virus, while fearing an epidemic,
    (E) virus, the fear of an epidemic,

19. Nelson had just walked into the meeting and that was when he was told that his plan had finally been approved.

    (A) and that was when he was told
    (B) when he learned
    (C) when it was learned by him
    (D) and then they told him
    (E) and then he learned

20. A fascinatingly intricate web of canyons and plains on the surface of Venus may camouflage
          A   B   C   D
    two distinct continents. No error
                              E

6. WRONG WORD USAGE

Some sentences include a word or phrase that is wrong because it's not the correct word to use, as in the case of an incorrect preposition, adjective, conjunction, or other part of speech. In other sentences, a word is incorrect because it has the wrong meaning.

Example: In the evening, Sarah becomes preoccupied in her homework.

We don't get preoccupied "in" something, but "with" something.

Correct: In the evening, Sarah becomes preoccupied with her homework.

Example: Harrison always treated his mother very respectively because he admired her success.

"Respectively" means in corresponding order. The correct word is "respectfully."

Correct: Harrison always treated his mother very respectfully because he admired her success.

Exercise set 6: Wrong word usage

Choose the answer that results in a clear and concise sentence, free from awkwardness or ambiguity.

1. <u>Many of</u> Peter Paul Rubens' paintings were <u>inspired from</u> the religious turmoil in Germany
     A   B
   <u>during his</u> youth and <u>his travels</u> to Italy later in his life. <u>No error</u>
       C   D   E

2. One argument in favor of annual family reunions, which would include relatives from across the <u>state, because getting together</u> at other times is so difficult.

   (A) state, because getting together
   (B) state; because getting together
   (C) state, is that getting together
   (D) state is getting together
   (E) state, that is because to get together

3. <u>Having studied</u> extensively for the optometry examination, Raymond felt <u>capable to make</u>
          A   B
   distinctions <u>among</u> the various problems <u>associated with</u> the eyes. <u>No error</u>
                 C   D   E

4. Lacking the information to make an appropriate decision was why the local town council found it difficult to ensure the quality of the water supply.

    (A) Lacking the information to make an appropriate decision was why the local town council
    (B) Difficult to implement, the local town council lacked the information to make an appropriate decision and
    (C) Because of lacking the information to make an appropriate decision, the local town council
    (D) Lacking the information to make an appropriate decision, the local town council
    (E) Local town councilmen who lacked the information to make an appropriate decision and were finding it difficult to

5. Underneath the concrete foundation lies the original water supply pipes and drainpipes that
        A   B
    were installed when the house was built. No error
          C   D   E

6. The entire valley, along with several nearby towns, is visual to anyone willing to climb the
                          A   B C   D
    1,852 steps to the top of the tower. No error
                                          E

7. The traffic was so congested and the crowd so thick as the worried mother would not let go
                                              A   B   C
    of the child's hand for even a moment. No error
                        D   E

8. Most of Eli Whitney's cotton processing methods have been so generally adopted by other industries and as a result people no longer realize how original they were.

    (A) and as a result
    (B) resulting in the fact that
    (C) and therefore
    (D) that as a result
    (E) that

9. Many of Robert Wood's paintings were inspired from England's landscapes the painter
       A   B
    had seen before he emigrated to the United States in 1910. No error
       C   D   E

SAT Grammar—Prioritized

10. Although Anne Bronte's novels outsold those of her sisters, <u>she is less widely recognized for an author than</u> Emily and Charlotte.

    (A) she is less widely recognized for an author than
    (B) she is not as recognized for an author than
    (C) she is less widely recognized as an author than
    (D) she is less widely recognized for being an author than
    (E) she is less widely recognized for an author as

11. People are no more likely <u>to become</u> healthier <u>by reading</u> books on health and nutrition <u>as</u>
                            A   B   C
    they are to become <u>more athletic</u> by watching sporting events. <u>No error</u>
                          D   E

12. Although the Greeks <u>were</u> <u>among</u> the best navigators <u>of the Mediterranean</u>, as shipbuilders they
                            A   B   C
    were <u>not equal of</u> the Eqyptians. <u>No error</u>
            D   E

13. An ardent abolitionist, Elizabeth Cady Stanton is also remembered as a well-known <u>advocate for women's rights, when she presented her</u> Declaration of Sentiments at the Seneca Falls Convention in 1948.

    (A) advocate for women's rights, when she presented her
    (B) advocate for women's rights, when she had presented her
    (C) advocate for women's rights; she presented her
    (D) advocate for women's rights, although she presented her
    (E) advocate for women's rights, she presenting her

14. In her new book, *Lulu's Trail*, <u>that</u> recounts her experiences hiking the Appalachian Trail, Marit
                                             A
    Janse <u>examines</u> the reasons for the trail names <u>people are given</u>, profiling such characters
            B   C
    <u>including</u> Snacker, Lone Wolf, Miles, and Bella. <u>No error</u>
       D   E

15. One striking feature of John Ford's films is he used stock company actors, actors who worked on contract with a movie studio.

    (A) he used
    (B) how it used
    (C) when he used
    (D) the use of
    (E) by using

16. The MP3 player is a relatively recent invention, while it may soon make CDs obsolete.

    (A) The MP3 player is a relatively recent invention, while it
    (B) Being that it is a relatively recent invention, the MP3 player
    (C) The MP3 player is a relatively recent invention that
    (D) The MP3 player, although a relatively recent invention, they
    (E) Because the MP3 player is a relatively new, and, as such, it

17. Cameras have been installed at major intersections in most major cities; these are used primarily in the catching of vehicles running red lights.

    (A) primarily in the catching of vehicles running red lights
    (B) primarily to catch vehicles running red lights
    (C) primarily in the catching of vehicles that run red lights
    (D) primarily for the purpose of catching vehicles running red lights
    (E) primarily to catch vehicles that run red lights

18. The defense attorney, noticing the nervousness of the witness, compared his testimony at the trial to his original statement and concluded that his testimony was inconsistent to his original statement.

    (A) concluded that his testimony was inconsistent to his original statement
    (B) concluded that his testimony was inconsistent with his original statement
    (C) had concluded that his testimony was inconsistent to his original statement
    (D) concluded that his testimony was being inconsistent with his original statement
    (E) concluded that his testimony had been inconsistent to his original statement

19. Many teachers were alarmed by the school board's ruling that gave principals <u>discretionary power to determine about having classrooms monitored</u> by the administrative staff.

    (A) discretionary power to determine about having classrooms monitored
    (B) discretionary power to determine about monitoring of classrooms
    (C) discretionary power to determine about classroom monitoring
    (D) discretionary power to determine whether classrooms should be monitored
    (E) discretionary power to determine if they should monitor classrooms

20. In the opinion of the professor, <u>reading</u> the first five novels <u>in the series</u> <u>is</u> not necessary
                                                     A   B   C
    <u>in the enjoyment</u> of the sixth. <u>No error</u>
           D   E

7. COMMA SPLICES/RUN-ON SENTENCES

There are two common errors when punctuating two sentences that are closely related:
    a) Comma Splice
    b) Run-on

a)   **Comma Splices**

Two complete sentences (independent clauses) must be separated by punctuation stronger than a comma. We use a comma to separate a dependent clause from an independent clause, but for two independent clauses we use either a semi-colon or a period.

Example: Sally canceled her trip to Yosemite National Park, she learned that her mother had become very ill.

Both of these clauses can stand alone, making this a comma splice. We can fix this in at least three ways.

1)   Replace the comma with a semi-colon.

    Sally canceled her trip to Yosemite National Park; she learned that her mother had become very ill.

2)   Make two complete sentences.

    Sally canceled her trip to Yosemite National Park. She learned that her mother had become very ill.

3)   Add a subordinating conjunction to one of the clauses.

    Sally canceled her trip to Yosemite National Park because she learned that her mother had become very ill.

b)   **Run-ons**

Even worse than a comma splice is a run-on or fused sentence. In this case, two sentences are run together with no punctuation.

Example: Kevin parked in the back row of the parking lot he wanted to protect his car from scratches.

This is two complete sentences strung together with no punctuation separating them. This can be corrected in any of the three ways shown above.

Exercise set 7: Comma splices/run-on sentences

Choose the answer that results in a clear and concise sentence, free from awkwardness or ambiguity.

1. Early in his career, Henri Cartier-Bresson wandered around the world with his <u>camera, eventually, his work made</u> the field of photojournalism recognized as legitimate.

    (A) camera, eventually, his work made
    (B) camera; eventually, his work made
    (C) camera; eventually, his work making
    (D) camera, but later, eventually, to make
    (E) camera, therefore, eventually, his work made

2. The best photographs in the exhibit <u>intrigue, they catch</u> the viewer between the eccentric and the normal.

    (A) intrigue, they catch
    (B) intrigue, but they catch
    (C) intrigue which catches
    (D) intrigue: they catch
    (E) intrigue; it catches

3. One of the first women in the United States <u>to be granted</u> a patent was
                                                    A
   <u>Sarah Mather, her invention</u> of a submarine telescope and lamp <u>permitted</u> sea-going vessels
            B   C
   <u>to survey the depths</u> of the ocean. <u>No error</u>.
            D   E

4. The Fair Labor Standards Act of 1938 outlawed employment of children under the age of fourteen, primarily farms were affected during the next few years.

    (A) primarily farms were affected during the next few years
    (B) children not working on farms not affected during the next few years
    (C) primarily children working on farms were affected during the next few years
    (D) but the act primarily affected farms during the next few years
    (E) but applying primarily to farms during the next few years

SAT Grammar—Prioritized

5. Sally Ride, the first female astronaut, <u>attended Stanford University, she was a double major in physics</u> and English, receiving degrees in both subjects 1973.

   (A) attended Stanford University, she was a double major in physics
   (B) attended Stanford University, where she was a double major in physics
   (C) attended Stanford University, she majored in both physics
   (D) attended Stanford University, a double major in physics
   (E) who attended Stanford University, and she was a double major in physics

6. In the 1996 Atlanta Olympic games, the United States gymnastics team <u>took</u> the <u>gold,</u>
                                                                                                           A   B
   <u>they became</u> known <u>as</u> the Magnificent Seven. <u>No error</u>
       C   D   E

7. The Robert Frost Farm, near Derry, New Hampshire, was home to the popular poet Robert <u>Frost; today, it is</u> a popular attraction offering tours, displays, and poetry readings.

   (A) Frost; today, it is
   (B) Frost, thus making it
   (C) Frost, now being
   (D) Frost; today,
   (E) Frost, it is now

8. The opponents of the bill to regulate speed limits on the waterway <u>were few</u> but
                                                                                                             A
   <u>influential enough</u> to prevent <u>its</u> <u>being passed</u> in the Senate. <u>No error</u>
          B   C   D   E

9. The new medical school at Lake Nona is accepting applications from across the <u>nation, there will be</u> 45 places in the inaugural class.

   (A) nation, there will be
   (B) nation, it will have
   (C) nation, and there would be
   (D) nation; with
   (E) nation for the

10. The report on the research belongs less to the land of knowledge than to <u>that of speculation, the writer has given us</u> more imaginings than fact.

    (A) that of speculation, the writer has given us
    (B) those of speculation, the writer has given us
    (C) that of speculation, the writer had given us
    (D) that of speculation; the writer has given us
    (E) that of speculation, the writer has given to us

11. Most familiar artists are talented in <u>only a single field, William H. Macy, however, is notable</u> as an actor, director, screenwriter, and teacher.

    (A) only a single field, William H. Macy, however, is notable
    (B) only a single field, but William H. Macy is notable
    (C) only one field, William H. Macy, however, is notable
    (D) only a single field, William H. Macy, however, has been notable
    (E) only a single field, however, William H. Macy is notable

12. I will do the Savage Seven <u>in December it is seven marathons</u> on seven consecutive days.

    (A) in December it is seven marathons
    (B) in December, seven marathons
    (C) in December, it is seven marathons
    (D) in December it was seven marathons
    (E) in December, which consists of seven marathons

13. I hope to hike the Grand Canyon <u>next summer, I'll hike from the North Rim</u> to the South Rim on the first day, and then return to the North Rim on the second day.

    (A) next summer, I'll hike from the North Rim
    (B) next summer, from the North Rim I'll hike
    (C) next summer; I'll hike from the North Rim
    (D) next summer, so I'll hike from the North Rim
    (E) next summer, I'll be hiking from the North Rim

SAT Grammar—Prioritized   91

14. Many African plants have been used to treat common ailment for centuries, some are now used in Western medicine as well.

   (A) have been used to treat common ailment for centuries, some are now used
   (B) were used to treat common ailment for centuries, some are now used
   (C) have been used to treat common ailment for centuries, some of them are now used
   (D) have been used to treat common ailment for centuries, there are some now used
   (E) that have been used to treat common ailment for centuries are now used

15. In 1903 Aida de Acosta, at the age of nineteen, hopped into a dirigible in Paris, she became the first woman to fly solo in a powered aircraft.

   (A) hopped into a dirigible in Paris, she became
   (B) hopped into a dirigible in Paris, she was becoming
   (C) hopped into a dirigible in Paris, she then became
   (D) hopped into a dirigible in Paris, becoming
   (E) hopped into a dirigible in Paris,

16. Because Dixie Crossroads, a popular restaurant in Titusville, FL, draws such large crowds, it is
                               A   B   C
    highly recommended to call ahead for Priority Seating. No error
                         D   E

17. Georgi Golakov was intending to study aeronautical engineering, he came to the United States from Bulgaria to do that.

   (A) Georgi Golakov was intending to study aeronautical engineering, he came to the United States from Bulgaria to do that.
   (B) Georgi Golakov was intending to study aeronautical engineering, he came to the United States from Bulgaria.
   (C) Georgi Golakov came to the United States from Bulgaria to study aeronautical engineering.
   (D) Georgi Golakov was intending to study aeronautical engineering, when he came to the United States from Bulgaria to do that.
   (E) Having come from Bulgaria to the United States, Georgi Golakov was intending to study aeronautical engineering.

18. No photographer ever <u>fully expects</u> to capture <u>completely</u> the character of his <u>subject, this</u>
                                    A   B   C
    picture of the queen <u>is</u> no exception. <u>No error</u>
                           D   E

19. <u>College students can greatly benefit from having internships, these often lead to permanent jobs.</u>

    (A) College students can greatly benefit from having internships, these often lead to permanent jobs.
    (B) College students can greatly benefit from having internships, which often lead to permanent jobs.
    (C) College students could greatly benefit from having internships, these often lead to permanent jobs.
    (D) College students can greatly benefit from having internships while in school, permanent jobs often result from these.
    (E) College students can greatly benefit from having internships, these can often lead to permanent jobs.

20. Some Japanese gardens, <u>such as</u> zen gardens and rock gardens, <u>are designed</u> to create peaceful
                                            A   B
    <u>surroundings, people</u> find these gardens <u>conducive to</u> meditation. <u>No error</u>
               C   D   E

8. WRONG COMPARISONS

In sentences in which two things are compared, be careful that the two things are like. For example, we can't compare a person to a time period.

Example: American novelists of the early nineteenth century wrote in a different style than most English novels of the same period.

The sentence is comparing novelists to novels. We can either compare novels to novels or novelists to novelists.

Better: American novelists of the early nineteenth century wrote in a different style than most English novelists of the same period.

Exercise set 8: Wrong Comparisons

Choose the answer that results in a clear and concise sentence, free from awkwardness or ambiguity.

1. Allison has read every book Gabriel Garcia Marquez <u>has written</u> , <u>and she</u> <u>considers</u> no other
                                                                           A   B   C

   novels as interesting <u>as he is</u>. <u>No error</u>
                               D   E

2. British rock music of the 1960s and 1970s was often more stylistically innovative than <u>American rock musicians of the same period.</u>

   (A) American rock musicians of the same period
   (B) Americans whose rock music was of the same period
   (C) that of the same period by Americans
   (D) the same period of American rock music
   (E) American rock music of the same period

3. <u>Recognizing that</u> a delay <u>would be an advantage</u>, the chairman postponed the vote but
               A   B

   requested that the board continue to meet <u>until when</u> the remaining issues were
                                                                     C

   <u>satisfactorily decided</u>. <u>No error</u>
           D   E

4. Clear evidence that merchants are trying hard <u>to meet</u> the demands, <u>however frivolous,</u>
                                                    A   B
   of consumers, <u>is found</u> by comparing the cereal and juice sections of a supermarket today
                      C
   <u>with years ago</u>. <u>No error</u>
          D   E

5. The nutritional outcomes of using traditional chemical fertilizers consisting of nitrogen, phosphorus, and potassium are less effective than <u>organic fertilizers</u>.

   (A) organic fertilizers
   (B) with organic fertilizers
   (C) those of organic fertilizers
   (D) when organic fertilizers are used
   (E) if one uses organic fertilizers

6. In the middle of the nineteenth century, American surveyors created maps <u>that were</u>
                                                                                A
   <u>much more accurate</u> than <u>previous mapmakers</u> <u>because of dramatic</u> improvements in surveying
            B   C   D
   tools and techniques. <u>No error</u>
                              E

7. The wings of birds and bats are actually modified front legs, but <u>being unlike birds, bat wings</u> are webbed rather than feathered.

   (A) being unlike birds, bat wings
   (B) bats' wings, unlike birds' wings,
   (C) by being unlike birds, bats' wings
   (D) bats' wings, and unlike birds' wings,
   (E) bat wings are unlike bird wings,

8. Most American diners in the 1990s <u>ordered more whole grain dishes than</u> the 1970s and 1980s.

   (A) ordered more whole grain dishes than
   (B) have ordered more whole grain dishes than did
   (C) ordered whole grain dishes more than the foods of
   (D) ordered more whole grain dishes than with the American diners in
   (E) ordered more whole grain dishes than did American diners in

9. No one will weaken the reputation of our tutoring center like Ashley's departure.

    (A) No one will weaken the reputation of our tutoring center like Ashley's departure.
    (B) No one will weaken the reputation of our tutoring center like Ashley's departure will.
    (C) Ashley's departure will weaken the reputation of our tutoring center like none other.
    (D) The reputation of our tutoring center will be weakened by Ashley's departure more than any.
    (E) Nothing will weaken the reputation of our tutoring center as much as Ashley's departure will.

10. Unlike the case with Rani, who was tired after working all weekend, I wanted to go to
                 A   B   C
    the rally to hear the gubernatorial candidate's speech. No error
               D   E

9. DISAGREEMENT IN NUMBER

Pay attention to quantities, especially when referring to people. Consider this sentence:

Example: People who wish to become a model should be aware that modeling isn't as glamorous as many think.

People don't make "a model," but "models." Likewise, football players don't make a role model; they make role models.

Exercise set 9: Disagreement in number

Choose the answer that results in a clear and concise sentence, free from awkwardness or ambiguity.

1. In recent years, trial lawyers <u>are relying on</u> psychologists to help them <u>predict how</u> particular
                                             A   B
   kinds of people <u>will behave</u> as <u>a member</u> of a jury. <u>No error</u>
                  C   D   E

2. <u>There are</u> dozens of charitable organizations headed by celebrities, <u>but these</u> well-known
       A   B
   people are, <u>in most cases</u>, nothing more than <u>a figurehead</u>. <u>No error</u>
                  C   D   E

3. <u>Much of</u> the success of Stanley Kubrick and Steven Spielberg <u>as a director</u> of science fiction
      A   B
   movies has been <u>attributed to</u> their knowledge of the technical work necessary
                        C
   <u>to make such</u> films. <u>No error</u>
       D   E

4. After comparing features, <u>Joe thought that the prices of either of the refrigerators were a bargain.</u>

   (A) Joe thought that the prices of either of the refrigerators were a bargain.
   (B) Joe thought that the prices of either of the refrigerators was a bargain.
   (C) Joe thought that the price of each of the refrigerators was a bargain.
   (D) Joe thought that the prices of either one of the refrigerators was a bargain.
   (E) Joe thought that the prices of both of the refrigerators was a bargain.

5. The ice skaters, after training for many years, hope <u>to win a place on the Olympic team to thus become a competitor</u> at the highest level of their sport.

   (A) to win a place on the Olympic team to thus become a competitor
   (B) they will win places on the Olympic team, and thus become a competitor
   (C) that they will win a place on the Olympic team to thus become a competitor
   (D) to win places on the Olympic team, thus they will become a competitor
   (E) to win a place on the Olympic team and thus become competitors

6. There <u>are</u> three candidates for mayor, <u>two of whom</u> <u>have</u> recently served as <u>a member</u> of the
         A   B   C   D
   county commission. <u>No error</u>
                          E

7. <u>As young women</u>, Emily Bronte <u>wrote</u> novels <u>along with</u> her sisters Anne and Charlotte, all
      A   B   C
   well known <u>for</u> their widely read books. <u>No error</u>
              D   E

8. The local television station <u>cited</u> both the stormy weather and the lack of enthusiastic
                                  A
   campaigning <u>as a reason</u> for the <u>unexpectedly poor</u> turnout in the <u>most recent</u> election.
                  B   C   D
   <u>No error</u>
      E

9. The beagle <u>is possibly</u> a little more nervous <u>than</u> the Laborador, but either of these dogs
                 A   B
   <u>would make</u> <u>an excellent pet</u> for a family with small children. <u>No error</u>
        C   D   E

10. Both of the candidates <u>running for</u> senator had been <u>an accountant</u> before going into
                              A   B
    politics, <u>yet</u> they disagreed on several issues <u>related to</u> economic policy. <u>No error</u>
              C   D   E

10. ADVERBS (usually missing "ly"

When reading the sentences, be careful to read only what is there. It is easy to "autocorrect" and supply a missing "ly" for an adverb.

Example: The water in the stream was moving more slow than usual because there had been little rainfall recently.

The water was moving "more slowly," but if you expect the phrase "more slowly," you might not notice that the "ly" is missing.

Exercise set 10: Adverbs (usually missing "ly")

Choose the answer that results in a clear and concise sentence, free from awkwardness or ambiguity.

1. Just when the editorial board thought things were going <u>smooth</u> at the newspaper, a crisis
                                                                     A

    erupted that <u>brought about</u> <u>changes in priorities</u>, including <u>increased attention to</u> international
                        B   C   D

    affairs. <u>No error</u>
              E

2. In recent years, the number of women <u>who</u> are pharmacists, a group <u>at one time</u>
                                            A   B

    <u>almost exclusively</u> male, has <u>rapid</u> increased. <u>No error</u>
         C   D   E

3. <u>Even though</u> tragedy usually portrays profound messages about humankind, comedy has
      A

    sometimes <u>been</u> taken <u>just as serious</u> <u>as tragedy</u>. <u>No error</u>
                 B   C   D   E

4. The completion of the task was delayed by the <u>unexpected</u> power failures, <u>although</u> the work
                                                     A   B

    schedule had been as carefully laid out <u>as</u> it <u>was suppose to be</u>. <u>No error</u>
                                              C   D   E

5. Just when the staff thought everything was going <u>smooth</u> at the television station, a catastrophic
                                                       A
   event <u>occurred</u> <u>that brought</u> about changes in <u>both</u> priorities and staff assignments. <u>No error</u>
           B   C   D   E

6. Even though comedy can convey <u>philosophical</u> messages about humankind, solemn drama <u>has</u>
                                       A   B
   usually <u>been taken</u> <u>more serious</u> than comedy. <u>No error</u>
              C   D   E

7. Neither the program guide <u>nor</u> the <u>docent</u> explained the background of the stained glass pieces
                                A   B
   <u>thoroughly enough</u> to <u>satisfy</u> inquisitive visitors. <u>No error</u>
           C   D   E

8. The story <u>told by</u> Filipino Jemuel Kalalo of a <u>seeming random</u> crime that <u>ensnares</u> the
                A   B   C
   lives of several strangers <u>is</u> impossible to forget. <u>No error</u>
                                D   E

9. In *Through the Ivory Gate*, Rita Dove <u>writes</u> <u>lyrical</u> about Virginia, <u>who</u> <u>recounts</u> her
                                             A   B   C   D
   coming-of-age story. <u>No error</u>
                            E

10. After Linda caught the cat on the kitchen counter, the cat scurried into <u>its</u> bed <u>as quick as</u>
                                                                                A   B
    it could when Linda <u>began</u> <u>spraying</u> water on him. <u>No error</u>
                            C   D   E

11. CORRELATIVE CONJUNCTIONS

Some conjunctions work in pairs, such as either-or. A thing is *either* attribute A *or* attribute B. For example, it cannot be either-and, nor can it be neither-or.

Common pairs of correlative conjunctions are:
    either-or
    neither-nor
    both-and
    between-and
    as-as
    at once-and
    not only-but also

Exercise set 11: Correlative conjunctions

Choose the answer that results in a clear and concise sentence, free from awkwardness or ambiguity.

1. A healthy business can be measured not only by the growth of sales <u>but it has an</u> emotional effect on its employees.

    (A) but it has an
    (B) as well in the
    (C) but also by the
    (D) also the
    (E) in the way of having an

2. The Athabascan people, <u>one of</u> the Native American cultures in Interior Alaska, not only
                          A
<u>practice</u> respect for all living things <u>and also</u> <u>believe in</u> sharing natural resources. <u>No error</u>
  B   C   D   E

3. He emerges <u>from</u> this biography as a mercurial figure <u>whose</u> impulsiveness is <u>as likely</u> to lead
              A   B   C
his company into disaster <u>than to</u> propel it to new levels of success. <u>No error</u>
                          D   E

4. Although Marcia <u>had made</u> a commitment to finish writing the book <u>by</u> August, she had
      A   B
neither the energy <u>or</u> the inclination to continue <u>working</u> on it. <u>No error</u>
                              C   D   E

5. The Seminole tribe <u>acted</u> as a single nation not only in establishing domestic policies <u>and also</u>
                                   A   B
<u>in making</u> <u>both</u> trade alliances and treaties. <u>No error</u>
       C   D   E

6. Although Charlotte <u>had made</u> a promise to complete the large mural <u>by</u> September, she had not
                                 A   B
considered the weather <u>or</u> the delay in <u>receiving</u> her shipment of specialized paints. <u>No error</u>
                                      C   D   E

7. During any one workout, most runners <u>choose between speed or endurance because</u> it is nearly impossible to work on both at the same time.

   (A) choose between speed or endurance because
   (B) choose between speed and endurance because
   (C) choose between speed or endurance since
   (D) choose either speed and endurance because
   (E) have chosen between speed or endurance because

8. Developing <u>exceptional</u> skills in Tai Chi <u>requires</u> not only abundant physical <u>proficiency</u>
                        A   B   C
<u>as well as</u> a large measure of mental discipline. <u>No error</u>
       D   E

9. W. E. B. Dubois is an important historical figure not only because he helped establish the National Association for the Advancement of Colored People (NAACP) <u>but he, unlike</u> Booker T. Washington, insisted on full civil rights and increased political representation.

   (A) but he, unlike
   (B) but also because he, unlike
   (D) but he, who unlike
   (D) but because he was also,
   (E) but he was, unlike

10. Even though Surya's parents wanted her to decide on a major soon, the decision was made more difficult because she was as talented at architectural design than she was at music.

    (A) because she was as talented at architectural design than she was at music
    (B) because her talent was a great at architectural design than it was at music
    (C) because she was about as talented at architectural design than she was at music
    (D) because she was equally as talented at architectural design than she was at music
    (E) because she was as talented at architectural design as she was at music

12. COMPARATIVE VS. SUPERLATIVE

When we compare exactly two things, we use the words *fewer*, *less*, *more*, and other descriptors ending in "er." When we compare three or more things, we use the words *fewest, least, most*, and other descriptors ending in "st."

Examples: Of the two actors, the *older* one is also the *taller*.
Of the five French horn players, Bobby produced the *smoothest* tone.

Both of these sentences are correct. In the first, "older" and "taller" are correct because two people are being compared. In the second, we are comparing Bobby's tone to four others, so "smoothest" is correct.

Exercise set 12: Comparative vs. superlative

Choose the answer that results in a clear and concise sentence, free from awkwardness or ambiguity.

1. According to no <u>lesser of an authority than</u> Norman Hastings, the most momentous event in the early history of the United States of America was the Louisiana Purchase.

    (A) lesser of an authority than
    (B) lesser an authority such as
    (C) less of an authority as
    (D) less of an authority than was
    (E) less an authority than

2. Of the many lakes in the United States, Oregon's <u>brilliant blue Crater Lake is one of the more</u> colorful.

    (A) brilliant blue Crater Lake is one of the more
    (B) Crater Lake, which is brilliant blue, is the more
    (C) brilliant blue Crater Lake is one of the most
    (D) brilliant, blue Crater Lake is more
    (E) Crater Lake is brilliant blue, plus most

3. Of my two daughters, Melissa is older, but Megan is tallest.

   (A) Melissa is older, but Megan is tallest
   (B) Melissa is oldest, but Megan is taller
   (C) Melissa is older, but Megan is taller
   (D) Melissa is older, but then Megan is tallest
   (E) Melissa is the oldest, but Megan is tallest

4. More college students are choosing majors in the social sciences, <u>but degrees based on mathematics and science lead to careers that pay the most</u>.

   (A) but degrees based on mathematics and science lead to careers that pay the most
   (B) but degrees based on mathematics and science lead to careers that pay the more
   (C) but with the degrees based on mathematics and science lead to careers that pay the most
   (D) but degrees based on mathematics and science lead to those careers that pay the most
   (E) but degrees based on mathematics and science lead to careers, which are the ones that pay the most

5. The <u>younger</u> of three children, Anna <u>began</u> playing violin at the age of five and soon
          A   B
   <u>surpassed</u> her two <u>older</u> siblings in musical ability. <u>No error</u>
      C   D   E

6. Eleanor Roosevelt <u>used</u> her position as First Lady <u>to promote</u> social reform <u>more than</u> either
                        A   B   C
   Lou Henry Hoover <u>or</u> Grace Coolidge. <u>No error</u>
                     D   E

7. Because it is so difficult to get accepted by most colleges, <u>Jackson High School is preparing its students to be the more highest qualified graduates</u> in the state.

   (A) Jackson High School is preparing its students to be the more highest qualified graduates
   (B) Jackson High School is preparing its students to be the highest qualified graduates
   (C) Jackson High School is preparing their students to be the more highest qualified graduates
   (D) Jackson High School is preparing its students to be the most highest qualified graduates
   (E) Jackson High School is preparing its students to be the more higher qualified graduates

8. Raphael Patrick's latest book, <u>depicting</u> a young boy's coming of age in Ireland <u>during</u> the
                                 A   B
   1960s, is <u>even</u> more <u>livelier</u> than his earlier books. <u>No error</u>
           C   D   E

9. The company found that <u>its</u> profits <u>were growing</u> <u>more stronger</u>, with an improved
                                 A   B   C
   outlook and more opportunities <u>for promotions</u> for its employees. <u>No error</u>
                                          D   E

10. A comparison of Theodore's essay to Madeline's essay shows that <u>Theodore's contains the most specific examples to support his thesis</u>.

    (A) Theodore's contains the most specific examples to support his thesis
    (B) Theodore's contained the greatest number of specific examples to support his thesis
    (C) Theodore's contain the most specific examples to support his thesis
    (D) Theodore's contains more specific examples to support his thesis
    (E) Theodore's contains the greater specific examples to support his thesis

13. NOTES ON ESSAY WRITING

The essay contributes about one third to the total Writing score, with Writing Multiple Choice contributing two thirds. This is why I believe it is more productive to learn the grammar concepts that are tested and work toward improving the Writing Multiple Choice sections. However, many colleges are looking at the essay score by itself.

The essay is read by two readers, each of whom gives it a score of 1-6. The two scores are added together to produce a score of 2-12. It appears that a total score of 8 or higher is satisfactory. It also appears that a majority of students received a total score of 8—a 4 from each reader.

Here is my advice for how to achieve a high score on the essay.

1. Read the quote two or three times. Then read the question at least 3 times. Be sure you understand exactly what the question is asking.

2. Every prompt I've seen can be answered "yes" or "no." Take three to five minutes to brainstorm what examples you could use for each position. The longer list will tell you which position to take. For example, I might react initially by thinking I want to answer "yes." But if I can think of only one example to support "yes," and I can think of three examples to support "no," then clearly I should take the "no" position.

3. State your position clearly in the first paragraph, using two to three sentences. You might also refer to the examples you intend to use.

4. Don't worry about the number of paragraphs. This essay does not need to conform to the typical 5-paragraph essay structure.

5. Use a lot of detail in your examples. In other words, don't be too brief or too vague. Be very specific. Don't be afraid to use more than one paragraph for one example.

6. Given the choice between another example and the concluding paragraph, I think you should write another example. From the essay scores I've seen, the more examples, the better.

7. Think through each sentence before you begin writing it. It's easy to start with a good phrase, but then get lost trying to finish the sentence.

8. Don't try to use big words unless these words are a part of your normal vocabulary. If you make an effort to use "SAT" words, your sentence is likely to be awkward and it will sound forced.

Good luck with your essay!

APPENDIX A: BASIC GRAMMAR DEFINITIONS

Main parts of Speech:

Name	*Definition*	*Examples*
noun	name of a person, place, or thing	book, thought, lake, dentist
pronoun	refers to or takes the place of a noun	I, you, he, they
verb	shows action or a state of being	they *walk*, we *write*, it *is*, there *are*
adjective	word that describes a noun	*blue* shirt, *tall* building, *fast* car, *excited* children
adverb	word that describes a verb, adjective, or other adverb	walked *quickly*, speak *logically*, *unusually* fast, calls *frequently*
preposition	a connecting word that shows the relationship between two nouns or between a verb and a noun	book *on* the table, walked *in* the door, spoke *with* the man
conjunction	a word that connects nouns, phrases, clauses, or sentences.	
	Coordinating conjunctions connect elements of equal rank.	apples *and* pears, pencil *and* paper
	Subordinating conjunctions connect clauses of unequal rank.	*Although* I'm late, I'll … *If* Sara goes, I'll … *Because* it was raining, Tim decided…
	Correlative conjunctions appear in pairs.	*Either* the green *or* the purple … *Both* tasty *and* healthy… *Not only* the cat *but also* the dog…
direct object	the receiver of the action shown by the verb	The boy hit the *ball* out of the park.
indirect object	the receiver of the direct object	Greg gave *Sally* the papers. gave…papers to Sally

APPENDIX B: ANSWERS TO EXERCISES

Exercise set 1-A: Identifying subjects and verbs. For ease in reading, subjects are underlined with a dotted line and verbs are underlined with a solid bold line.

1. Although the exact **cause** of the fever **was** never **determined**, modern **doctors** now **believe** that **Helen suffered** from meningitis.

2. **Conflicts** between mining operations and environmentalists **have** repeatedly **arisen**, causing Congress to reconsider legislation **that prohibits** mining within habitats of endangered species.

3. The senator's **staff is** persuaded that the **announcement** of the investigation, coming just days before the filing deadline, **was calculated** to discourage the senator from running for reelection.

4. For the remainder of her life, **Annie Sullivan continued** to encourage Helen's appetite for learning, providing a constant light in Helen's otherwise impenetrable darkness.

5. By today's standards, Kennedy's medical **problems were** severe enough to qualify him for federal disability or retirement.

6. Although **I did** not **get** my usual summer tan in Toronto, the **warmth** of the people there more than **made** up for what the **climate lacked**.

7. Her father found odd jobs that provided food and shelter for the family, but she never felt at home—and she never felt truly safe.

8. Despite the fact that they had traveled with hundreds of other refugees, her family was suddenly alone with strangers who spoke an unintelligible language.

9. On her first day of school, many children pointed, waved, and smiled at her, but she did not understand what they said.

10. People who dislike cats sometimes criticize them for being aloof and independent; people who are fond of cats often admire them for the same qualities.

11. The starling is such a pest in rural areas that it has become necessary to find ways of controlling the growth of its population.

12. No matter how cautiously snowmobiles are driven, they are capable of damaging the land over which they travel.

13. Since there are two pencils, a pad of paper, and a ruler on each desk, students do not have to bring their own supplies.

SAT Grammar—Prioritized   115

14. By virtue of their size and supersensitive electronics, modern radio telescopes are able to gather more waves and discriminate among them with greater precision than earlier versions could.

15. Soon after the arrival of the first visitors, many residents of the remote island thought it possible that the outside world, instead of being frightening, could be fascinating and worth exploring.

16. It was a large painting and I realized as soon as it arrived at my home that however much I loved it I had no wall and no room in which to display it properly.

17. Aviation belonged to the new century in part because the engineering that went into flying machines was utterly different from that of the Industrial Revolution.

18. By attracting new industry when the old factory closed, the commissioners kept the economy of the town from collapsing.

19. Simi and Phillip were inspired to become professional writers after hearing a famous author speak about the challenges of historical research.

20. Air pollution caused by industrial fumes has been studied for years, but only recently have the harmful effects of noise pollution been explored.

Exercise set 1-B: F: Subject-verb agreement	Exercise set 1-C: Incorrect use of "ing" verbs	Exercise set 1-D: Verb tense: wrong tense, shift in tense, past/past perfect tense	Exercise set 1-E: Missing verb, incomplete sentence	Exercise set 1- Active/passive verbs
1. C	1. C	1. D	1. D	1. B
2. B	2. D	2. E	2. A	2. D
3. D	3. E	3. B	3. B	3. D
4. E	4. D	4. E	4. C	4. C
5. A	5. A	5. B	5. E	5. E
6. D	6. B	6. E	6. B	6. C
7. B	7. B	7. E	7. B	7. D
8. C	8. E	8. D	8. A	8. D
9. E	9. C	9. B	9. D	9. C
10. A	10. B	10. C	10. C	10. B
11. D	11. D	11. D	11. B	11. E
12. D	12. A	12. D	12. E	12 C
13. E	13. B	13. A	13. B	13. E
14. C	14. B	14. E	14. C	14. B
15. B	15. E	15. E	15. C	15. B
16. B	16. A	16. C	16. D	16. C
17. E	17. D	17. B	17. C	17. A
18. D	18. E	18. E	18. E	18. B
19. C	19. C	19. A	19. E	19. D
20. E	20. B	20. D	20. C	20. E

SAT Grammar—Prioritized

Exercise set 2-A:
Pronoun/antecedent agreement

1. D
2. D
3. E
4. D
5. B
6. E
7. C
8. B
9. D
10. E
11. E
12. B
13. D
14. B
15. D
16. E
17. B
18. C
19. C
20. D

Exercise set 2-B:
Unclear pronoun reference

1. D
2. E
3. C
4. A
5. B
6. E
7. E
8. ....
9. B
10. D
11. C
12. A
13. D
14. B
15. D
16. B
17. D
18. C
19. B
20. C

Exercise set 2-C:
Shift in point of view

1. A
2. D
3. C
4. D
5. C
6. B
7. B
8. E
9. E
10. D
11. E
12. C
13. E
14. C
15. D
16. C
17. D
18. B
19. C
20. A

Exercise Set 2-D:
Nominative vs. objective case

1. C
2. B
3. C
4. B
5. D
6. B
7. D
8. E
9. C
10. D
11. C
12 E
13. B
14. C
15. E
16. D
17. E
18. A
19. B
20. D

Exercise set 2-E: Unnecessary pronoun or no antecedent	**Exercise set 2-F:** Relative pronouns: whom, which, that, when, etc.	**Exercise set 3:** Dangling or misplaced modifiers	**Exercise set 4:** Parallelism	**Exercise Set 5:** Wordy, awkward, or illogical construction
1. E	1. D	1. B	1. C	1. E
2. B	2. C	2. C	2. B	2. C
3. E	3. A	3. C	3. D	3. E
4. E	4. D	4. D	4. C	4. D
5. C	5. C	5. B	5. C	5. C
6. E	6. E	6. D	6. C	6. E
7. B	7. B	7. D	7. D	7. E
8. C	8. B	8. D	8. B	8. D
9. B	9. D	9. B	9. E	9. B
10. D	10. E	10. D	10. A	10. B
11. D	11. E	11. C	11. B	11. D
12. B	12. C	12. C	12. C	12 E
13. C	13. B	13. E	13. C	13. D
14. E	14. B	14. C	14. B	14. E
15. D	15. B	15. B	15. C	15. C
16. B	16. C	16. D	16. D	16. B
17. C	17. C	17. D	17. E	17. E
18. A	18. C	18. C	18. E	18. C
19. B	19. D	19. E	19. A	19. B
20. D	20. D	20. D	20. C	20. E

SAT Grammar—Prioritized

Exercise Set 6: 10: Wrong word use	**Exercise Set 7:** Comma splices, run-ons	**Exercise Set 8:** Wrong comparisons	**Exercise Set 9:** Disagreement in number	**Exercise Set** Adverbs (usually missing "ly")
1. B	1. B	1. D	1. D	1. A
2. C	2. D	2. E	2. D	2. D
3. B	3. B	3. C	3. B	3. C
4. D	4. D	4. D	4. C	4. E
5. B	5. B	5. C	5. E	5. A
6. C	6. B	6. C	6. D	6. D
7. B	7. A	7. B	7. A	7. E
8. E	8. E	8. E	8. B	8. B
9. B	9. E	9. E	9. E	9. B
10. C	10. D	10. A	10. B	10. B
11. C	11. B			
12. D	12. E			
13. C	13. C			
14. D	14. E			
15. D	15. D			
16. C	16. E			
17. E	17. C			
18. B	18. C			
19. D	19. B			
20. D	20. C			

Exercise set 11:
Correlative conjunctions

Exercise set 12:
Comparative vs. superlative

1. 1.
2. 2.
3. 3.
4. 4.
5. 5.
6. 6.
7. 7.
8. 8.
9. 9.
10. 10.

www.ingramcontent.com/pod-product-compliance
Lightning Source LLC
Chambersburg PA
CBHW081457040426
42446CB00016B/3285